S0-BAY-094

THE MINISTRY OF THE

Christian School Guidance Counselor

By James W. Deuink

BOB JONES UNIVERSITY PRESS
GREENVILLE, SOUTH CAROLINA 29614

The Ministry of the Christian School Guidance Counselor
by James W. Deuink

© 1985 Bob Jones University Press, Inc.
Greenville, South Carolina 29614

ISBN 0-89084-273-6

Printed in the United States of America

20   19   18   17   16   15   14   13   12   11   10   9   8   7   6

Contents

Figures

Part I

to the Administrator

1 Defining the Term

Pupil personnel services cover a broad range of essential school support activities that can be categorized under eight basic headings: orientation, curriculum study, educational and vocational planning, child study and placement, informational services, counseling, job placement, and follow-up program. Closely associated with these basic activities is the compilation of accurate, complete historical student records.

The demand for these services grew out of the recognition of individual student needs and out of the concern expressed by those interested in the students' potential and progress (parents, teachers, prospective employers, college admissions personnel and other professionals). Despite the needs, however, the following historical examination shows that these educational services developed slowly and that once developed the specific duties became centralized in one person—the guidance counselor.

During the Colonial period, children were thought of as miniature adults. No special consideration was given to the concept of individuality, and all who were educated were educated alike. Not until after the Civil War did the concept of individual differences become part of educational planning. Some schools began to offer programs with more than one track, giving students the option of fast or slow progress based on their individual abilities.

Until the turn of the twentieth century, however, one basic curriculum was offered by most schools. Though the specific curriculum of each school varied, it was extremely uncommon for a school to offer more than one curriculum emphasis. But in the early 1900s the sufficiency of a singular curriculum was questioned. America was expanding, becoming more mobile and increasingly complex. Children no longer inevitably entered the family profession. Young people wanted direction for choosing their individual vocations; and since the traditional family counselors—the doctor, pastor, or respected relative—were not trained to give such counsel, the need for vocational guidance and training emerged.

Theodore Roosevelt is credited with focusing national attention on vocational training. In an article written for *Good Housekeeping* (November 12, 1908) Roosevelt stated: "Our system of public education should be so broadened in its scope as to include not merely the traditional cultural studies . . . but also instruction relative to the farm, the trades, and the home." Roosevelt demanded that the schools not only provide a broader curriculum but also provide more information about the working world. He believed that students ought to have a clear understanding of the options available to them after graduation. Others who supported Roosevelt in this early development of vocational guidance were Frank Parsons, Jessie B. David, Anna Y. Reed, Eli W. Weaver, and David S. Hill.

Concurrent with this development in vocational training was the development of standardized group psychological tests. Alfred Binet, a French psychologist, and his associate, Theodore Simon, first introduced a group intelligence test to the public in 1905. A revised version, published in English in 1916 and introduced in the United States by Lewis M. Terman of Stanford University, rapidly became popular. The needs of the military in World War I also stimulated research and development in this field.

In the 1920s and 1930s organized school guidance programs became more common, especially on the secondary level. Besides several administrative duties, the secondary counselor also became responsible for maintaining discipline and attendance records. Since that time, the basic tasks of the secondary school counselor have changed little.

During this time, guidance programs likewise developed on the elementary level. Elementary guidance personnel were usually concerned with counseling, child study, psychotherapy, pupil assessment, and parental aid. They were generally considered by administrators as less essential than secondary guidance personnel.

After World War II, the guidance movement significantly changed, for the writings of Carl Rogers influenced education during this period. Until Rogers appeared on the scene, the emphasis was on testing; after Rogers, it became counseling. Some educators say that Carl Rogers was to the counseling movement what Henry Ford was to the automobile industry. Rogers gave a totally new direction to the field by introducing the concept of nondirective counseling. As a humanistic psychologist, Rogers resisted the concept of absolute truth. He viewed truth as relative, and, therefore, believed that the counselor was not to offer advice from the perspective of "right" or "wrong." According to Rogers,

2 Recognizing the Need

Working with young people requires a basic understanding of how they think, act, and establish their priorities. Every age group has its own particular set of problems, and young people of school age are no exception. Eventually any school offering a full range of grades will encounter the sins inherent in our culture, even the most sordid sins. Thus, we should remember before beginning our discussion that the quality of a school is not determined by the problems the students have, but rather by how the school handles these difficulties.

Adolescence

Though children of all ages have problems, the most serious challenge school officials encounter are the problems involving adolescents—that turbulent age from about twelve to eighteen years.

Writers characterize this group in several ways, but there are two characteristics common to most descriptions: dramatic changes in physical development and an intense desire for independence. Almost without exception, any trait uniquely connected with adolescence could be placed under one of these headings.

Physical Development

Physical development is a fact of life, and when young people fail to develop as we think they should, we become disturbed. Why then is this specific change so unsettling? There are several reasons.

First, these physical changes occur much more rapidly than other physical changes, excluding, of course, those changes that occur during the first few months of life. Life's early changes, however, are not as threatening as those of adolescence. In a short time a child develops adult characteristics that he cannot use

lawfully. Though in other cultures this physical maturity is coincident with marrying and giving in marriage, this is not true in our culture.

Parents and others who have worked with this age group recognize the frustrations accompanying these dramatic physical changes. The specifics of these changes are beyond the scope of this book, and those who feel they may need a more detailed discussion should consult an adolescent psychology book. One significant point, however, is that psychologists now report that young people are experiencing puberty earlier than in the past. For school personnel, this means dealing with the difficulties of adolescence earlier and for perhaps a longer period of time.

Emotional Behavior

Emotional turmoil often attends this physical development. Certainly some of the turbulent behavior is a result of the hormonal changes linked with the physical changes, but why this period is typified by such erratic behavior is not fully understood. Some young people will experience more difficulty than others at this age. We are justfied, therefore, in tempering some of our responses to make allowance for the unusual stress they are encountering. We must remember, however, and instruct our young people that each individual is accountable for his own actions regardless of the external pressures and influences (Ezek. 18:4; Matt. 16:27; I Cor. 10:13; II Cor. 5:10; Heb. 4:12,13).

Problems of the Age

The physical and emotional burdens of adolescence are intensified by current trends. While there were, no doubt, past generations equally wicked, the acceptance of evil in this present age is without precedent in our nation's history.

For example, sexual promiscuity is an age-old sin; it was a problem in Noah's day and possibly earlier. However, in the United States between the years 1970 and 1982 the number of one-parent families with a *never married* head of household rose 367 percent. During the same period illegitimate births to teens increased from an annual rate of 199,900 to 271,801. It was reported that 33 percent of births to white teenagers and 86 percent of births to black teenagers were illegitimate. Obviously, in our culture there is little shame associated with illicit sexual conduct. Many would now concede that there is nothing wrong with sex outside marriage between consenting adults. But what are the reasons for this blatant decline in public morals, and how does this decline affect our young people?

Removal of Natural Barriers

In years past, young people were somewhat restrained from unwholesome relationships with the opposite sex by the threat of pregnancy and venereal disease. However, legal abortions in "respectable" clinics, easy access to various birth control devices, and the availability of free private counsel and treatment for minors without consent or knowledge of parents have done much to remove these natural barriers to illicit sexual relationships. Our age of "enlightenment" has made it possible for the "educated" and the "cautious" to partially avoid the consequences of their sin. Such activity still, however, takes its toll on a young man or woman, for many of the teenagers who indulge in fleshly sins are virtually consumed by guilt.

How can we use this information to help the young people entrusted to our care? Sexual temptations are especially alluring for the adolescent, and Christian adolescents are no exception. Satan will undoubtedly try to take advantage of their vulnerability. This problem is complicated because even the most discreet parent cannot completely shield his young person from a worldly emphasis on sex. It is used to sell everything from cosmetics to soda pop, making it increasingly difficult for the teenager to maintain a pure thought life.

As Christian educators we cannot ignore this problem. We must be aware of the terrible effects produced by an unwholesome thought life and deal directly with the problem. Providing a solid biblical emphasis on male/female relationships is a necessity. This is not to advocate instruction in the mechanics of sex or birth control, but rather to encourage scriptural teaching about the proper place of the marriage relationship in God's order of things. Unfortunately, much of the instruction given our young people is either too specific in its treatment of physiology or too vague in its application of biblical principles. We cannot expect them to remain untainted by the world's view unless we indoctrinate them with God's view.

Emphasis on Individual Rights

The strong concern for individual rights pervading our society has also contributed to its general moral deterioration. Man, in his effort to assert his independence from God, has concluded that there are no moral limitations on personal behavior as long as that behavior does not harm another individual or force him to do something contrary to his will. Rock music writers, advertisers, and others have promoted this amoral philosophy by encouraging individuals to be guided by pleasure. They refuse to acknowledge any absolute standard for conduct; there is, therefore, a complete lack of direction. Many young people are trapped in this vacuum, and even Christian young people are often unknowingly influenced by these attitudes.

For almost everyone, adolescence is a period of weaning away from parents and developing independence in thought and action. Young people who do not accept the standard of morality espoused by their parents frequently challenge their authority during this period. This is especially true if the young person perceives inconsistency between what his parents claim to believe and the way they act. On the other hand, if the young person recognizes a genuineness and sincerity in his parents' beliefs, he is more likely to submit to their authority even if he disagrees with their standards.

All young people are to be subject to the authority of their parents (Exod. 20:12; Eph. 6:1-3). Among the periods of development, adolescence offers the greatest challenge to parental authority. Harnessing and directing a young person's growing independent spirit is difficult. However, parents who have been faithful in rearing their children in the fear and admonition of the Lord (Gen. 18:19) may rely on God's promises to keep their children (Prov. 22:6). Parents, however, who have led inconsistent lives, have been frequently rebellious, or only reluctantly obedient (II Chron. 25:2) face serious difficulties and may lose their children. God does not delight in the death of the wicked (Ezek. 18:20-28), but neither does He force Himself on any, not even on the children of Christians. Parents who have failed to follow God's Word in training their children are unable to claim many of the promises God intended for their help and comfort during difficult times.

Emergence of the Drug Culture

Illegal drugs are one of the more serious problems facing the youth of today. Alcohol and tobacco, though still a threat, have been overshadowed by more dangerous and harmful drugs that have the capacity to cause insanity or continuing hallucinations. Though not all users react to drugs this violently, *some* do. We have all heard of young people who have died after a single drug experience, and of others who have committed suicide or murder while under the influence of such substances. Researchers tell us as many as 65 percent of today's youth, at one time or another, experiment with drugs. We must help our young people understand that no Christian has the right to "experiment" with drugs. They should be emphatically taught that indulging in any substance that harms the body or impairs the mental processes is a sin against the Holy Ghost (I Cor. 6:19,20; II Cor. 6:16).

Disregard for the Sanctity of Human Life

As a nation we have lost respect for the sanctity and value of life itself. This is best shown by society's attitude toward abortion. Many without Bible convictions are duped into believing that what is "legal" is also right. But the murder of an unborn, defenseless child is as wrong as the murder of the mother, and the simple fact that the parents request the abortion and the doctor condones the action does not make it right. Murder is never right in God's sight. The specific disregard for the life of an unborn child ultimately results in a lessening of concern for life generally. This attitude is simply one more evidence of man's attempt to usurp God's authority, and those who support such practices give tacit consent to the humanistic philosophy that man is his own master.

The rise of these ungodly attitudes has not gone unnoticed by our young people. They wonder why Christian adults allow such challenges to God's authority to go unquestioned. They reason that if adults have the right to conveniently choose to accept or reject God's authority in one area, they too have the right to make such choices. We have taught them this logic by example, the most powerful teacher of all.

Deterioration of the family

Young people are also confused by the deterioration of the family. The United States Census Bureau recorded that the divorce rate in America doubled between 1965 and 1976. The world certainly offers no standard for adolescents to follow. Unfortunately, many professing Christians are not giving them any better example.

We know that the family was the first institution established by God (Gen. 1:27, 2:23-25) and that a man's responsibility to his family is second only to his responsibility to God (I Tim. 5:8). Since Christ likens the relationship between man and wife to His relationship to each believer (Eph. 5:22-23), what do young people think when they see marriage vows set aside by their Christian leaders (Mal. 2:14)? Are spiritual commitments only a matter of convenience? Are we allowed to set aside God's commands when other people or things capture our attention? If so, though we claim to espouse Christian beliefs, our actions belie our words.

Leadership's Responsibility

In many respects the world is reeling out of control morally. Today's generation of young people were reared by parents whose parents were reared "according to Spock." Permissiveness coupled with a general lack of appreciation for God's Word prevails in many Christian homes. Unfortunately, our young people are largely following in the footsteps of parents who are wholly committed to the pursuit of pleasure and self-indulgence. The pull of the world is powerful, and for those who yield to the world's temptations, the fruit of sin follows as surely as night follows day (James 1: 14, 15). A genuine Christian school can help students, as well as their families, to see their spiritual needs and can guide them in finding God's answer to those needs.

Providing Spiritual Guidance

The involvement of Christian young people with the sins of the world, as distasteful as it is, is not their most serious problem. They are meddling with a far more basic problem. Though man was created to bring honor and glory to God (Isa. 43:1,7), in his natural state he rebels against his Creator (I Sam. 15:23). Unless our young people understand and accept God's claim on their lives, our efforts are futile.

Christian schools seeking to work with young people from worldly homes are fighting an uphill battle. Young people from nominal Christian homes present a similar challenge. Even those from godly families are so tainted with the presence of worldliness that they are difficult to preserve for God's glory. We face a tremendous struggle. Part of succeeding in this struggle rests in recognizing our enemy and the signs of his presence.

The curse of "easy believism" is one hindrance barring our young people from realizing their responsibility to God. The world has been sold a false bill of goods about the gospel and God's will for believers. Mass evangelistic efforts and local churches patterning their ministries after them have produced converts who continue in their sinful, self-serving pursuits even after conversion. Young people have been affected by this movement to a greater degree than their parents, and the result of these shallow spiritual experiences is that such young people are more difficult to disciple than those who have never come into contact with the gospel. We must teach them that repentance is an essential ingredient to personal salvation. We must guide them in understanding that a "new creature" in Christ forsakes the world and seeks to glorify God in word and deed (II Cor. 5:17).

Training for God's Service

The Word of God is consistent in its teaching from Genesis to Revelation—God's desire is to have a called-out people who, of their own volition, will choose Him not only as Saviour but also as Lord of their lives (I Sam. 12:19-25). Few Christian young people, however, are responding to God's call for service. The lure of the world and material gain are stronger than their desire to serve. Churches without pastors, mission fields without missionaries, classrooms without teachers and various other unfilled ministries vividly testify to this fact. While we realize that not all our young people will be called into what we refer to as full-time Christian work, far more are called than are responding. It is our duty to challenge them about the needs in God's vineyard and to give them direction in using their talents for their Lord. We cannot hope to convince them of the necessity and privilege of Christian work, however, if we are personally unfaithful to the call God has given to us.

Although this discussion of the problems of youth has not been exhaustive, it does represent the problems school administrators and other personnel encounter. The key to solving these difficulties is to recognize that all problems are spiritual and that every spiritual problem has a biblical solution. Our goal is to assist parents in training their children to be conformed to the image of Christ (Prov. 22:6, Rom. 8:29). Our concern is that our students develop not only physically and intellectually but also spiritually. If they do not, we have failed to fulfill our chief goal. As the following chapters will show, the counseling ministry can help us reach this goal, for it serves a twofold purpose: to help our young people avoid spiritual pitfalls (I Cor. 10:13; Heb. 2:18) and to aid those who have fallen prey to Satan's devices (Jer. 3:22; Hos. 14:4; Eph. 4:32; I John 1:9). Though such a ministry is by no means easy, it is spiritually valuable, and God has promised to be faithful to us as we are faithful to Him (I Thess. 5:24).

3 Meeting the Need

Having established the need for a counseling ministry in the Christian school, we will now look at the addition of the counselor to the school's professional staff and his subsequent role once he has assumed this position. The model envisioned calls for a professionally trained and/or experienced counselor who will pursue his responsibilities on a full-time basis.

Ideally any one of the following factors could justify the timely addition of a counselor to your staff:

- an elementary school with a student body of 500 or more students
- a conventional school with all twelve grades and an average enrollment of 25 or more students per grade
- a secondary school with grades seven through twelve or nine through twelve with an enrollment of 30 or more students per grade.

Those thinking only of the traditional guidance counselor's responsibilities may question the justification of a full-time position based on the above enrollments. However, as Figure 3.1 shows, the guidance counselor is viewed as a member of the school's administrative team. This is probably the most significant difference between the Christian school counselor and his public school counterpart. As you will see through later discussion (chapters 4-13), we assume that the Christian school counselor's training will not only enable him to counsel students, but also prepare him to perform several administrative duties commensurate with pupil personnel services. The combination of these routine counseling responsibilities with appropriate administrative duties justifies the position. By combining these duties the selected enrollments provide not only sufficient activities for the counselor's full-time employment, but also adequate financing for his position.

Figure 3.1

Suggested Organizational Structure

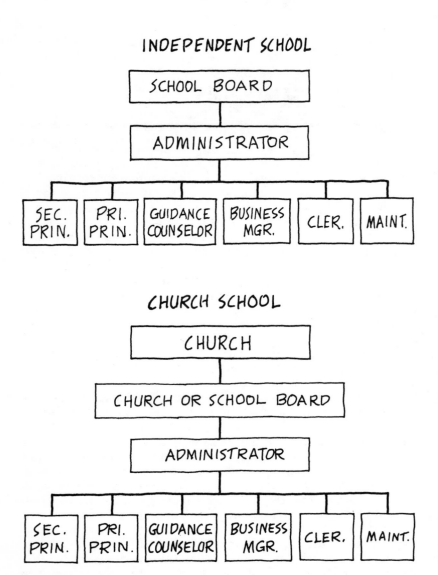

Qualifications of the Counselor

Preparation

Every position of Christian service requires preparation. Once the Lord has given us a burden for a particular ministry we must be careful not to rush ahead of Him and endeavor to meet the need through the strength of the flesh. Consider the nation of Israel in Egypt. Undoubtedly God was moved by their cries of anguish. This is evidenced by the fact that He called Moses and placed in his heart a desire to meet Israel's needs. But the implementation of God's plan to free His people was not immediate, for Moses was not fully prepared for this laborious task. The Lord took forty more years to equip His servant for leading the people. Administrators, then, should hardly become frustrated if God takes a few years to train His servants for effective service.

This caution inevitably leads to the question: "What specific preparation is necessary for the counseling ministry?" There is, of course, a considerable difference between what is ideal and what is minimally acceptable. Though this discussion will focus on the ideal, many schools will not be able to start out in this way.

The best preparation for the potential guidance counselor is an undergraduate degree from a Christian college with a major in education. Though an individual with training only in Bible could function effectively as a general counselor, he would not be adequately trained to handle the remaining administrative and clerical duties. The advantages of obtaining this education from a Christian institution cannot be overemphasized. Humanistic philosophy pervades the behavioral sciences, and too often a student can be subtly influenced by these ungodly attitudes. Consequently, a Christian seeking to enter the field of counseling from a secular educational background must be thoroughly familiar with the Word of God and able to filter out the humanistic philosophy from his training.

Following the completion of his undergraduate education, it is preferable for the student to teach while or before working on a graduate degree in pupil personnel services or in counseling from a Christian college. Some aspiring counselors may prefer to go directly from an undergraduate program into a full-time graduate program. They should be advised, however, that teaching is an invaluable complement to graduate training and would thus greatly benefit them.

Classroom experience is a necessary prerequisite to the counseling ministry. Whether this experience is obtained on the elementary or secondary level is not important, though teaching the specific age group the counselor desires to serve would prove most helpful. Exactly how much teaching experience is needed is a subjective judgment and will depend somewhat on the quality of the teaching experience and the size of the school where the potential counselor begins his counseling career. Teaching will help him understand not only the structure of your school, but also the process of education within the school. He will thus be better prepared to make effective contributions to the professional staff. An ineffective teacher is not likely to be an effective guidance counselor. It is wise, therefore, when considering counseling applicants with experience to check their references carefully.

Characteristics

As administrator there are several qualities you should look for in a counselor. The first and most important is that he be a genuinely spiritual person. Since the counselor will most likely deal with your young people on a more personal, intimate level than any other member of the school staff, his interest in them and their problems should exceed the level of interest expected of a classroom teacher. This interest in the students will be evidenced through his compassion for them (Jude 22).

A good guidance counselor should also be perceptive. Many times a young person in trouble will talk around his problem and never come to the point of what is actually bothering him. A counselor, therefore, must be able to perceive such evasive strategy and tactfully bring the student around to focusing on his real problem.

The counselor must also be trustworthy. Details of situations shared in confidence should remain confidential. There is perhaps no more sure way for a counseling ministry to fail than to have a counselor who is unable or unwilling to keep confidences.

Finally, the counselor must be a good example. His life must be consistent with the biblical advice he shares with others. The family of the married counselor should demonstrate the principles set forth for the Christian family in the Word of God. The husband and wife must have a good relationship with one another—the husband being the spiritual leader in the home, and the wife in subjection to her husband. Children must be respectful and obedient to their parents, showing spiritual maturity commensurate with their age. The family should be active in the local church and a good testimony in the community. Briefly stated, the counselor and his family should measure up to the standards given by Paul to Timothy (I Tim. 3).

The following guidelines will prove helpful in evaluating applicants for the guidance counseling position.

Figure 3.2

Guidelines for Selecting the Christian School Guidance Counselor

Spiritual

1. Must be born again.
2. Must be an active member of your church or another church of like faith and practice.
3. Must agree without reservation to your church's statement of faith.
4. Must evidence spiritual maturity.

Educational

1. Must have a bachelor's degree with a major in some area of elementary or secondary education, preferably from a Christian college.
2. Should have or should be willing to begin work on a master's degree, preferably in pupil personnel services, counseling, or Bible.

Experience

1. Experience is desirable; however, people with experience in counseling in Christian schools are rare. Lack of experience should not eliminate an individual from consideration if other criteria are met.
2. Experience in a Christian school setting is preferable to counseling in a public school setting or counseling outside the educational profession.

Personal

1. A married counselor would normally be preferable to a single counselor because of the additional experience that the individual would bring to the position.
2. The counselor's entire family must have a good testimony in the church and community.
3. The candidate should be able to identify some specific evidence of a calling and gifts in counseling.

Role of the Counselor

The Bible does not often deal in specifics of organizational matters. Little, for example, is said about the internal operation of the church. Likewise, the Bible does not deal with the operational procedures of the school. Scripture does provide for us useful principles, however, by which to govern these organizations.

One of Scripture's basic operational principles is orderliness (I Cor. 14:40). God is never the author of confusion. Consequently, a sense of order should be evident in the administration of our Christian schools. Each professional staff member should be properly trained for his position and his duties should be clearly defined.

The delegation of authority and responsibility to competent personnel is essential if your school is to maintain this principle of orderliness. Delegation is difficult, however, unless there is a proper evaluation of the school's work load and a realistic plan to hire qualified staff to carry that load. If the school fails in these areas, one of two things will happen: either the existing staff will be overburdened from attempting to absorb all the necessary duties or these duties will be delegated to untrained personnel. In either case, the effectiveness of the school suffers.

Figure 3.3 shows the many duties that can be effectively handled by a person trained in pupil personnel services.

Figure 3.3

Suggested Duties for the Christian School Guidance Counselor

Administrative Duties

1. Assist with general supervision and administration of the school
2. Serve as liaison for the church staff working with school families
3. Direct the orientation of students, parents, and teachers
4. Participate in in-service training
5. Interview prospective students and their parents
6. Assist the administrator with admissions decisions
7. Make curriculum recommendations
8. Prepare the master schedule

Counseling Duties

9. Administer school testing program
10. Interpret test information for students/parents/teachers
11. Assist teachers in the identification and understanding of student limitations
12. Help students plan their academic progress
13. Counsel students with academic problems
14. Provide vocational information
15. Help students make decisions about advanced education
16. Help students prepare for admission to other schools
17. Conduct student/parent/teacher conferences
18. Counsel students with discipline problems
19. Counsel parents of students with discipline problems
20. Counsel students with attendance problems
21. Provide general counsel to students
22. Provide general counsel to parents of students
23. Assist with follow-up activities

Clerical Duties

24. Prepare statistical reports
25. Maintain student records
26. Determine academic eligibility
27. Prepare student transcripts and recommendations
28. Clear students for graduation and academic awards
29. Conduct student registration
30. Assist students in finding employment

You will notice that these responsibilities include not only general counseling tasks, but also important administrative and clerical duties. This is the primary reason the guidance counselor is placed in an administrative position. (See figure 3.1.) He can be a valuable asset to your administrative team and should receive compensation and authority in keeping with this role.

In this chapter we have proposed an organizational model that combines the delegation of administrative responsibilities with the needs of pupil personnel services. Though the following chapters will address the potential counselor, the discussion of his administrative, counseling, and clerical duties can help you visualize how he can specifically aid you the administrator. We recognize that the assignment of duties to round out the counselor's schedule is somewhat arbitrary. Your individual local needs and specific school personnel may suggest more appropriate delegations, but these changes can be made without destroying the purpose of the model.

Our primary concern is that Christian schools recognize the need for a counseling ministry. The born-again guidance counselor is a necessary part of reaching students, for the counselor has the opportunity of ministering to young people at a time when they are receptive to outside influence. Students desire spiritual guidance, career counseling, and advice about further education. These decisions involving their future are imminent, and they need trained personnel to help them make these decisions. Schools that fail to provide such services, therefore, are forfeiting one of their greatest opportunities.

Part II

to the
Potential Counselor

4 Informational Services/Orientation

A good Christian school administration anticipates the needs of its constituency and develops institutional objectives and directional policies to meet those needs. Establishing these objectives and policies, however, is only the beginning. Once developed, this information must be clearly communicated not only to those outside the school, but also to the students, parents, school staff, and—in a church school—the entire church membership associated with the school. This responsibility may be largely undertaken by you as guidance counselor. Initially the task may seem overwhelming, but it becomes manageable when broken down into smaller components. Let's first list briefly the essential information needing dissemination and then survey the most effective methods to carry out each task.

Necessary Information

- Educational philosophy
- Admissions standards
- Financial policies
- Description of the professional staff
- Curriculum
- Extracurricular activities
- Academic expectations
- Discipline policy
- Internal policies
- Evaluation of spiritual development
- Evaluation of academic development
- Vocational opportunities
- Opportunities for higher education
- Selecting and recommending appropriate educational institutions

Effective Methods

There are several effective methods to use in communicating important information. The three most basic methods are printed materials, personal interviews, and scheduled classes. Unfortunately, another commonly used method is the informal discussion. Though a certain amount of communication in this form is natural and unavoidable, a word of caution may be helpful.

A school that relies heavily on informal discussion as a primary means of communication will have little incentive to think through its program and will tend to react to situations as they occur and to rely on spontaneous decisions. The result of such decision making will be a lack of direction and consistency in implementing the school's philosophy. Two major problems will thus emerge: the school will lose control of the information communicated, and those reluctant to ask questions will proceed blindly. Under such circumstances the school will be unable to operate effectively and may, at times, run counter to its primary objectives.

Printed materials

There are two basic advantages to using the printed page. First, the information disseminated will be consistent and clear for anyone needing it. Second, it will be readily available for reference when a review of the details is appropriate.

The design of printed matter is important, for the way in which the information is presented conveys how important the institution believes it to be. The production of your materials should be carefully considered, whether the information is to be distributed to the general public or to be used only by the school staff. You will also find it profitable to develop a unique logo to use on all printed information. After a period of time the logo will serve as an immediate identification symbol to anyone who sees your material.

Another design consideration is the size and shape of your material. Most of the promotional material you produce will need to be mailed. It is therefore wise to design such materials so that they will easily fit into standard-size business envelopes. This design will make unnecessary the additional expense of specially prepared envelopes. It should be possible to mail letters, applications, advertising brochures, question/answer brochures, and student handbooks in envelopes used with the school's regular letterhead. Single-page documents should be designed on 8-1/2 x 11-inch stock. The handbook and other brochures should also be printed in a slender format about 8-1/2 x 3-1/4 inches.

Reference Materials

Besides the printed materials prepared by the school staff, there are also valuable reference materials that you as a counselor can make available to the school constituency. Such materials can aid students and parents in understanding the purpose and importance of Christian education. Guidance about further education, vocational opportunities, and aptitudes required for various jobs can also be obtained through these reference tools. The potential for the use of such material is almost limitless and should be used to the fullest extent. If your school has a bookstore, you should make certain that it is well stocked with a variety of these reference tools, and you should make it a point to regularly emphasize their availability and importance. If you do not have a bookstore, the materials could be made available at parent-teacher-fellowship meetings.

There are many other facets of the school that may interest the parents and students and could be communicated through printed materials. Those areas not included in the items previously discussed are a list of the professional staff and their academic credentials, the results of standardized mental ability and achievement tests, a description of the school's curriculum, and a list of the school's scheduled activities throughout the year. Some schools have found that it is valuable to record this information and distribute it in a monthly or quarterly newsletter.

Personal Interviews

As counselor, you should be readily available to promote Christian education generally and your Christian school specifically through personal interviews. This method provides invaluable opportunities and should not be taken lightly. Besides interviewing prospective students and their parents, you may also have opportunity to talk with those who are not immediately interested

in enrolling their children but are interested in investigating the goals and functions of Christian schools. Such inquiries should not be viewed as an imposition, but rather as an occasion to give a solid gospel witness, for the gospel is an integral part of explaining our purpose for Christian education.

Until you become experienced in conducting interviews, however, it is wise to follow a prescribed interview format. The purpose of this suggestion is to insure that you cover the information you want to cover. Remember that your objective is to communicate and to receive essential information. If the line of communication breaks down in either giving or receiving the information, therefore, your interview becomes unproductive, and it is difficult to reestablish the same conditions for another interview.

Scheduled Classes

Another common method of communication is scheduled classes. This method is particularly beneficial for seniors. Many schools offer a special course to address specific issues that will help the student after graduation. Topics discussed include finding God's will for your life, settling on a vocation, considering higher education, finding a life partner, serving the Lord in the local church, managing personal finances, and other pertinent subjects. Outside speakers are occasionally brought in, and special seminars are periodically scheduled to meet special needs.

Up to this point, we have given a general survey of the methods used in disseminating essential information. Let's now look at the specific ways in which these methods can be used to communicate your basic objectives to the general public and to aid you in orienting the students, parents, and professional staff of your school.

Communicating to the General Public

There are at least three printed items that you should prepare to promote your school's program to the general public. These are an advertising brochure, a question/answer brochure, and a student/parent handbook. A fourth item, a curriculum guide, is also highly recommended.

Advertising Brochure

The advertising brochure is often the school's first professionally printed material. It is tempting for a new or small school to reproduce this material on a photocopy machine, mimeograph, or spirit-master process. Though this approach may be simple and inexpensive, it is not advisable. Your advertising brochure may be the only document that many people use in deciding whether to consider your school. If it strikes them negatively, you may lose the opportunity to help them. This may seem unfair, but we must remember that the school brochure will fall into the hands of people you may never meet, and it may be the only impression they will ever have of your ministry. If you were in the used car business, your advertising brochure could perhaps have ink smears, crooked print, and misspelled words without damaging your credibility. But in the business of educating young people, if you do not know the difference between "a principle" and "the principal," you cannot expect people to trust you to teach their children.

The size of the school brochure is important. As suggested previously, you should plan all the promotional materials with distribution in mind. An 8-1/2 x 11-inch paper works well because it generally provides enough space for the information to be communicated and will fit into a standard-size envelope. Folded twice, it will provide six panels. One panel can be used to summarize the financial data, three panels on the opposite side can be used for the following general information: a brief history of the school, the admissions policy, required statement on nondiscrimination, curriculum, a small map identifying the school's location, a statement about discipline and conduct, your biblical/doctrinal position, statement of purpose, and the academic status of the school. The two remaining panels can serve as a front and back cover. See Appendix A for an example.

Question/Answer Brochure

Over a period of time it will be possible for you to identify the questions most frequently asked about your school. Organizing them in an orderly fashion and presenting a carefully reasoned response will provide you with an opportunity to impress on the public your school's willingness to give direct answers to important questions.

The question/answer brochure can be an effective tool, for it can allay probing questions that may be difficult for a new school to handle. The brochure will also help the public recognize the professional nature of your school. Difficult questions that you know you will be asked can be answered without duress, and much of the conflict that would be encountered can be avoided. A straightforward answer to a difficult but unasked question is disarming. The following are some of the questions frequently asked:

- Who sponsors your school?
- Why does your church have a school?
- Does your school accept government assistance?
- What makes your school different from other schools?
- How does your curriculum compare with public and other private schools?
- Are all students required to go to chapel? How often?
- What extracurricular activities are available at your school
- Is your school approved by the state? Is it accredited?
- Are your teachers and administrators certified?
- What is the academic preparation of your professional staff?
- How do your students perform academically?
- Do all of your students study Bible?
- Do you accept all students who apply at your school?
- Do your students have difficulty transferring to other schools?
- If my child graduates from your school, will he be able to go to any college he chooses?

A formal printed brochure is impressive, but if you are currently unable to handle the expense for this, the same results could be achieved by copying the questions and answers on to your school letterhead.

Though the preceding list of questions was prepared to be used with prospective students and their parents, a similar list could be prepared for currently enrolled students. Remember— information removes anxiety and prevents unnecessary resistance to institutional programs.

Student/Parent Handbook

The student/parent handbook is intended primarily for students and their parents as a reference on school policy. It can be an effective promotional tool as well, however. The handbook cannot possibly contain all the school's policies governing student/parent/teacher/school relationships, but it should cover the basic areas and be specific enough to establish the philosophical atmosphere of the institution. Those areas of school policy that are not specifically discussed should fit into the pattern established by the handbook. No student or parent who reads the handbook carefully should be taken completely by surprise by any policy that is not specifically discussed.

A complete breakdown of the content of a Christian school student/parent handbook may be found in Appendix B. It must be remembered that because of the uniqueness of each Christian school, a handbook must of necessity be highly individualized to be useful. Any attempt to put together a handbook simply by copying the collective efforts of others is bound to result in failure. The primary value of reviewing examples of other handbooks is simply to identify topics that need to be addressed.

It is easy for us when writing such materials to overemphasize the negative. But we should remember that the way we express our ideas in these materials establishes the tone of our school. A delicate balance between the negative and the positive must be maintained. Much of the sting of the negative emphasis can be relieved by providing explanations. Inappropriate behavior should be identified, and the subsequent disciplinary action discussed. Your handbook will be more productive if it conveys the belief that students desire to do right, and the thrust of your handbook should give them the information they need to fulfill your expectations.

Another important purpose for the handbook is to help parents understand what they can expect of the school. Though Christian educators admit that the school exists to help parents meet God's requirements in educating children, the school staff frequently fail to address the concerns of parents and appear puzzled by their questions. We must always keep in mind that Christian schools exist as a ministry not only to the child but to the parents as well.

Curriculum Guide

The fourth printed item every school should have is a curriculum guide. The curriculum guide should list every course offered at every grade level with a course description, an abbreviated list of objectives for the year, and a list of the instructional materials or at least the textbooks that will be used in each course. Making this guide available for public view will evidence the thorough preparation your school has made for the education of its students.

Orienting Students/Parents/Teachers

The task of developing policies and effectively communicating them to students, parents, and school staff cannot be done solely with printed material. Orientation meetings are another effective method of communication that can reinforce and clarify important information. Though the administrator is primarily responsible for overseeing these meetings, you as the counselor can assist him in performing the following duties.

Orientation of Students

All of us tend to forget things we view as irrelevant or inconvenient. Students are certainly no exception. We cannot expect children to have the same concern for the rules as the administration. Even though we have provided printed materials for the students, we cannot assume that they are familiar with everything we want them to understand. Some schools provide orientation sessions only for new students. Other schools provide sessions for the old students as well. A case can be made for either approach, but we believe it would be beneficial to have orientation meetings for all students each year.

Students (grades seven and above) should be required to read the handbook and may be given an examination on its contents. This emphasis on the content of the student/parent handbook will prove invaluable as the year progresses.

Orientation of Parents

Parents respond well to carefully planned, thorough orientation meetings. There is a direct correlation between the effort the school representatives put forth to explain the school program and the desire of the parents to cooperate. You should pay careful attention to how the parents respond and adjust future programs accordingly. A good orientation meeting is largely a matter of common sense, but this initial communication between parents and school staff will prove invaluable as the school year progresses.

Once school actually opens, there are many demands on the time of parents and school personnel. Consequently, most schools that conduct orientation meetings do so before school begins. If the school offers grades K-12, it is wise to have two or three meetings. Schools could consider having one meeting for parents of children K-8 and another for grades 9-12. Having more than one meeting will provide time for addressing the specific needs of each grade level and will shorten the meeting time. Much of this planning, however, will depend on the size of your school and how your grade levels are structured.

The content of the orientation meeting is important. Although it does not need to be entertaining, the content should be presented in an interesting way. The information should focus on helping parents understand what your school is doing, why you are doing it, how it will affect their children, and what specific problems they may encounter in the immediate future. The specific actions you expect them to take in assisting the school and in offering their direct support should be clearly explained, and those things you have noted as being problems in the past should be given the most attention.

Orientation of Teachers

Like students, faculty members tend to forget what seems irrelevant. Thus, like student orientation there should be a yearly session for both old and new faculty members. New faculty need a thorough indoctrination in school policy, and old faculty need to be reminded of things that have caused difficulties in the past.

All faculty members need to be well acquainted with the school's expectations for both students and parents. Failure to inform them properly will inevitably result in conflicts. Church schools should also be certain that the pastor is involved in orienting the faculty.

A carefully written faculty manual is essential to orient your staff properly. This is a document that needs constant revision. Your faculty manual may initially be small, but it will develop as the school and personnel increase. While you as a counselor may not be specifically responsible for preparing such a manual, you can provide beneficial assistance to the administrator. An outline for the contents of a typical Christian school faculty manual appears in Appendix C.

5 Screening Students for Admission

Once a basic admissions policy has been established you, the counselor, could greatly help your administrator by performing the routine screening of applicants. You are the logical person to assume these duties, for you are accustomed to reviewing academic credentials, using and interpreting standardized tests, evaluating student potential, and orienting students, parents, and teachers.

Reviewing Applications

Reviewing applications is the first step in screening applicants. A well-developed application like the one found in Appendix D can be an invaluable asset in this part of the admissions process. Such an application can help you weed out those who are not qualified for enrollment. Inquiries do not necessarily suggest that a person is genuinely interested in what you have to offer. Some people may simply be looking for an inexpensive private school. Others may be seeking a generally religious education but not a program that specifically seeks to conform the student to the image of Christ. Sometimes, the examination of the student's application will show past behavioral problems that could jeopardize other students. Some students may have physical or mental handicaps or learning disabilities that your school could not handle. Occasionally a student's religious background will run contrary to the school's philosophy. In all these cases, a well-prepared application will help you identify obviously unqualified or marginally qualified applicants.

Following this initial review of applications, you can determine which students are ineligible, which are eligible, and which will need specific administrative consideration. Under the assumption that an application requires a minimum of ten minutes to review and that one hundred applications have been received, you will

have saved your administrator two full days of work by undertaking this responsibility.

It may be wise to insert here some basic information about the admissions committee. Forming a committee responsible for making final admissions decisions is helpful. These decisions would be based, of course, on the established policy. For a church school this committee could consist of the counselor, the pastor, the administrator, the chairman of the deacon board, and a member of the school board. In an independent school the committee could be made up of the counselor, the administrator, and one other administrative staff member. In any case, the committee should have a minimum of three members and the total membership should be an odd number. The advantage of this system is that the pressure of disenchanted parents will rest on the committee rather than on an individual. Rejection of an application is easier for parents to accept if it is less personal.

Testing

Your next step in the admissions process may be either interviewing the student or testing the student. It is preferable, however, for testing to precede the interview since testing is an essential consideration in the final admissions decision.

Some may question the desirability of testing and the validity of using academic ability as a means of limiting enrollment. Few schools are large enough, however, to provide a program that can meet the needs of all students regardless of their abilities. Most schools, therefore, determine a range of abilities they can successfully accommodate and then develop an admissions policy that will limit their enrollment to the established range. We should remember that we do students a disservice if we accept them into our school when our curriculum is not equipped to meet their needs.

Standardized testing is the most effective means of identifying students' abilities. Figure 5.1 illustrates the use of standardized test scores to limit enrollment on the basis of academic achievement and mental ability. The chart in Figure 5.2 shows the relationship of the various types of standardized test scores to the normal curve.

Figure 5.1

Minimum Standardized Test Scores Required for Admission

To be accepted in grades two and above, students must make a minimum score on a standard entrance examination. Minimum scores are as follows:

a. An average score of 35 percentile or above on selected portions of the Stanford Achievement Test.

b. An average score of 30 percentile or above on selected portions of the Stanford Achievement Test and a score of 27 percentile (IQ 90) on the Otis-Lennon Mental Ability Test.

c. An average score of 25 percentile or above on selected portions of the Stanford Achievement Test and a score of 27 percentile (IQ 90) on the Otis-Lennon Mental Ability Test will permit consideration for admission at one grade below that applied for through the eighth grade.

d. Due to the accelerated academic program, students applying for grades nine and above that cannot qualify on the basis of points (a) or (b) cannot be accepted.

Figure 5.2

Standardized Test Scores and the Normal Curve

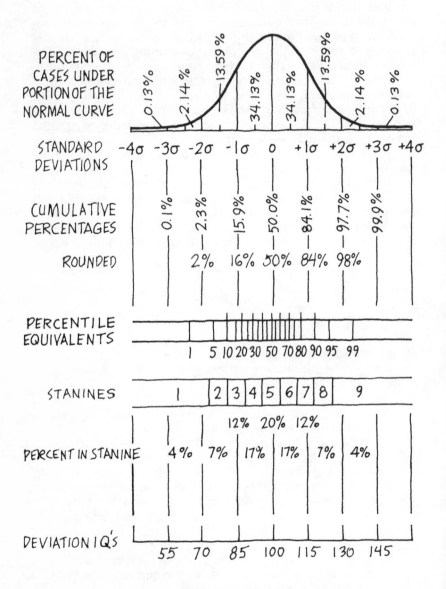

The same standardized achievement and mental ability tests used in the regular testing program should also be used for admissions testing. This will help the school personnel become familiar with the tests and enable them to make appropriate predictions about an applicant's prospects for success in school.

Scores developed by standardized achievement tests are expressed in three ways: stanines, percentiles, and grade equivalents. Of the three, percentiles are the easiest to understand. Mental ability tests are usually expressed in terms of IQ and percentiles. Since both tests use percentile scores, it is probably best to use percentiles when discussing test results with the parents and students. A more thorough discussion of testing is given in Chapter 8.

Figure 5.3 gives the distribution of marks to be expected in a normal distribution. In Figure 5.4 seven different levels of ability are identified based on the students' previous grade-point average and standardized test scores. An indication of the distribution of expected grades in each group is also given. The ability level of the group may apply to a particular class, a grade level, or the entire student body. By studying the performance of students in your school and comparing their standardized test scores, it will be possible to make reasonably accurate predictions of student potential.

Figure 5.3

Distribution of Marks Based on a Normal Population

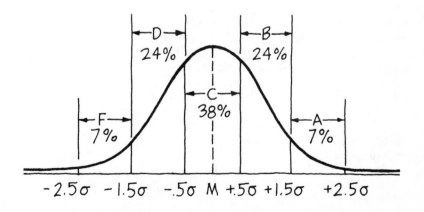

Figure 5.4

Letter Mark Distribution Statistics
at Seven Levels of Ability

Ability Level	Lower Limit of A's	Percent of Marks					Ability Measures	
		A	B	C	D	F	GPA	Percentile
Exceptional	0.7	24	38	29	8	1	2.80	79
Superior	0.9	18	36	32	12	2	2.60	73
Good	1.1	14	32	36	15	3	2.40	66
Fair	1.3	10	29	37	20	4	2.20	58
Average	1.5	7	24	38	24	7	2.00	50
Weak	1.7	4	20	37	29	10	1.80	42
Poor	1.9	3	15	36	32	14	1.60	34

From *Essentials of Educational Measurement* (p. 248) (3rd ed.) by R. L. Ebel, 1979, Englewood Cliffs, NJ: Prentice-Hall.

The testing schedule may vary from school to school. If there are several applicants, a specific time can be scheduled to test the entire group. Smaller schools may prefer to test students individually as they come for interviews, but if this approach is used, another meeting time must be scheduled to discuss test results. Thus, it is more realistic and professional to have admissions tests scheduled, conducted, and evaluated before the interview. But whether a student's test scores qualify him for admission or not, he and his family should be contacted for an interview. A knowledge and discussion of the test results will be of value to the student and his parents in making future decisions.

Schools that do not use academic ability as a means of limiting enrollment find testing helpful in tailoring their curriculum to meet general student needs. The type of testing administered and the specific tests used are an important consideration. To use an inappropriate test can be damaging, since the results may lead to wrong decisions.

Students ineligible for admission may be informed of the committee's decision by letter. The examples in Figure 5.5 may be helpful.

Figure 5.5

Sample Letters to Students Ineligible for Enrollment

Dear Parent:

Your application for your son John has been received and carefully considered. It is with regret that we advise you that he does not meet our admissions requirements at this time because of previous discipline problems in school. We will be able to reconsider this decision one year from now.

Your application fee is being refunded in full.

* * *

Dear Parent:

Your application for your son John has been received and carefully considered. It is with regret that we advise you that we will not be able to accept him at this time.

John's entrance examination scores were below the minimum established for acceptance. The entrance examinations are given to help us select students who will have the greatest opportunity for success in the school. Our program is academically competitive, and we have found that students who do not score above the minimum we have established are not generally able to do well in their studies here.

* * *

Dear Parent:

Your application for your son John has been received and carefully considered.

John's entrance examination scores do not meet the standards established for the grade level for which John applied. It does appear that he would be successful here if given the opportunity to make up academic deficiencies. We would be willing, therefore, to accept John for enrollment in the next lower grade level.

Please call the school office for an appointment to discuss this matter.

Those students who are eligible for enrollment should be advised by letter of the next step in the admissions process. The letter in Figure 5.6 is a sample of what may be used.

Figure 5.6

Sample Letter to Student Passing Initial Screening

Dear Parent:

Your son John's entrance examinations have been scored, and he appears to meet our academic requirements for admission. All students are required to have an admissions interview. At least one parent is required to attend the interview with the student. Both parents are urged to attend if possible. Please call the school office to schedule your interview.

Although form letters may be used for admissions tasks, the letters should be original. They should *never* be duplicated by mimeograph or spirit process or run off in quantity on a plain-paper copier. Both letters of rejection and acceptance should be kind and as warm as the circumstances permit. Larger schools are advised to consider purchasing memory typewriters or word processors for these tasks. This equipment will save much time, and since there are many other appropriate uses for this equipment in the school, the value will soon compensate for the initial cost.

Interview

In most Christian schools the administrator conducts most interviews, not necessarily because he chooses to do so but because there is no one else on the staff that can handle the responsibility. Again, as a professionally trained counselor, you are the logical person to fit this role.

Students and their families are important people. Consequently, much prayer and careful consideration should be given the decision to accept or reject a student. Remember that a good interview takes time. A minimum of twenty to thirty minutes should be allotted for each family, and if unusual problems are anticipated, additional time should be scheduled. The interview should take place in a physically comfortable environment that is as free from interruptions as possible. An interview guide like the one in Figure 5.7 should be prepared to insure that the meeting will be kept on track and that all essential information will be covered.

Figure 5.7

Sample Admissions Interview Guide

1. Be certain the application is completed. Every question must be answered, and the application must be signed.
2. Discuss and check off each of the following items:
   - ___Purpose of interview
   - ___History of school
   - ___Christian emphasis
   - ___Plan of salvation for parents who do not appear to be born again
   - ___Aim of the school
   - ___Curriculum information
   - ___Discipline policies and procedures
   - ___Student handbook
   - ___Tardiness and absence
   - ___Dress and hair
   - ___Student's attitude (emphasize for students above grade four)
   - ___Parents' cooperation
3. Review items to be turned in at office: supply fee, certificate of immunization, changes of address, and telephone numbers.
4. Remind parents that reservations are not held until all fees have been paid.
5. Parents' questions.

The admissions committee will need to decide if the admission decision will be given to the parents at the interview or by letter. If an admissions committee system is used, it is best to notify parents by letter. Figures 5.8 and 5.9 give you some examples.

Figure 5.8

Sample Letters of Rejection from the Admissions Committee

Dear Parent:

The admissions committee has carefully considered the application you have submitted for your son, John. We regret that we cannot approve his enrollment at this time.

The XYZ Christian School has been organized to assist parents with their God given responsibilities to "train up a child in the way he should go" (Prov. 22:6). On the basis of the application you have submitted and the personal interview conducted last Friday, the admissions committee believes that the goals of the school and those of your family are not compatible. Therefore, we do not believe the enrollment of John would be in our mutual interest.

We thank you for your interest in the school, and we trust you will find a private school whose purpose is more in keeping with your goals.

* * *

Dear Parent:

The admissions committee has carefully considered the application you have submitted for your son John. We regret that we cannot approve his enrollment at this time.

The XYZ Christian School has been organized to assist parents with their God given responsibilities to "train up a child in the way he should go" (Prov. 22:6). On the basis of the application you have submitted and our discussion of John's discipline problems, we do not believe it would be in the overall best interest of the school to accept John. While we are concerned about John and have a desire to help him, we must also consider the six hundred other students already enrolled in the school and the commitment we have to their parents. We will be willing to reconsider John's application next year.

Thank you for your interest in the school; we trust you will find a school that will be able to consider John's special needs at this time.

Figure 5.9

Sample Letter of Acceptance from the Admissions Committee

Dear Parent:

The admissions committee is pleased to advise you that your son John's application for enrollment in the fourth grade has been approved. We are pleased that you have selected the XYZ Christian School to assist you in training your child. We look forward to working with you in this important endeavor.

The first day of school is Monday, September 1. You will be receiving additional information in the mail. Please read it carefully. An invoice will be sent showing the amount and date of all payments due throughout the school year. Feel free to call the school office if you have any questions about your relationship with the school or our program.

We covet your prayers as final arrangements are made for the school year.

Established schools frequently receive more applications from qualified students than they can accommodate. Thus, a reasonable waiting list should be made and eligible students should be advised of their placement on the list. These lists should generally be no more than five students long for any one grade. It would be unfair to hold a student on a waiting list who could be actively enrolled in another school.

The personal interview with the student and his family is an extremely important part of the admissions process. Therefore, this critical task must be undertaken by someone like the counselor who is not only thoroughly familiar with the school's philosophy and policies but is also able to decide whether the student and his family agree with this philosophy and purpose. The decisions that result from these meetings will determine the overall character of your student body.

6 Curriculum Recommendations and Scheduling

Scheduling begins with an established academic policy and ends with a particular student walking into a specific classroom to take a specific course. Of necessity, any treatment of scheduling will require an initial discussion of curriculum development and of high school graduation requirements. Once the curriculum is developed, however, there will be basically four critical considerations that will determine your individual master schedule: course requirements, student needs, classroom availability and teacher availability.

Curriculum Decisions

Basic Curriculum

If you are working in a new or young Christian school, you may be in the position to develop the curriculum as well as to create the master schedule. Basically a Christian secondary school curriculum is built around the following subjects:

- *Bible:* should be required at every grade level.

- *English:* should be required at every grade level from seventh grade upward.

- *Social Studies:* should be required at the seventh-and eighth-grade levels and at least three of the four years of high school; there should be a solid emphasis on both world history and United States history as well as on state and local government.

- *Science:* should be required at the seventh-and eighth-grade levels and at least two of the four years of high school; college-bound students should have science every year.

- *Mathematics:* should be required at the seventh-and eighth-grade levels and at least two of the four years of high school; both college-bound students and vocationally-oriented students should be provided with mathematics courses appropriate to their future needs.

- *Fine Arts:* should make plans to provide instruction in music, speech, and art as the school grows.

Foreign language, physical education, and business education courses round out the curriculum. Student needs will vary from school to school and from community to community. Small schools must be cautioned to avoid the temptation to offer frill courses or even legitimate courses where the demand is insufficient or where the cost is too high for the school budget.

Additional Considerations

When educators first become involved in Christian education, they sometimes fail to consider what others in education are doing. They have the impression that to do things as others do, especially as public schools do, is unchristian. Our schools, however, are no less Christian if we offer United States history on the same grade level as the local public school. Nor are we less spiritual if we list a course as "United States History" rather than "A Christian History of America."

What distinguishes our Christian schools is 1) our underlying philosophy for the total school program, 2) the way we teach our courses, and 3) the content of our courses. There is usually no legitimate reason for a Christian school to fail to offer a regular, dependable core curriculum like the ones available in the neighboring public schools. To do so will make it easier for students to move from school to school and will give our Christian schools a wholesome image within the community.

It is also wise for you to obtain copies of your state and local graduation requirements and use them as a guide in establishing minimum requirements. Figures 6.1 and 6.2 show the present and future curriculum recommendations for South Carolina. The curriculum changes listed in Figure 6.2 are typical of the changes occurring across the country. Since many college entrance requirements now exceed curriculum offerings of Christian schools, you need to keep abreast of these changes and to keep your administrator advised of necessary curriculum changes.

Figure 6.1

Minimum Graduation Requirements for Public Schools in South Carolina as of the 1983/84 Academic Year

English	4 units
Mathematics	2
Laboratory Science	1
Social Studies (1 unit of U. S. History, at least 1/2 unit of government and at least 1/2 unit of economics)	3
Physical Education	1
Electives	7
	18 units

Source:
South Carolina Department of Education
Columbia, South Carolina

Figure 6.2

High School Course Requirements for Applicants to South Carolina Public Colleges and Universities Effective Fall 1988

Area	Units	
English	4	At least two having strong grammar and composition components, at least one in English literature, and at least one in American literature (completion of college preparatory English I, II, III, & IV will meet these requirements)
Mathematics	3	Including Algebra I & II; geometry is strongly recommended as the required third unit and a fourth unit is recommended but not required
Laboratory Science	2	At least one unit each of two laboratory sciences chosen from biology, chemistry, or physics; a third unit of a laboratory science is strongly recommended
Foreign Language	2	Two units of the same foreign language
Other	1	One unit of advanced mathematics or computer science or a combination of these; or one unit of world history, world geography, or western civilization
U.S. History	1	
Economics	½	
Government	½	
Additional Social Studies	1	
Physical Education or ROTC	1	

South Carolina Public Colleges
and Universities
at Which
New Requirements Will Be in Effect
FALL 1988

The Citadel	USC-Coastal Carolina
Clemson University	USC-Columbia
College of Charleston	USC-Lancaster
Francis Marion College	USC-Salkehatchie
Lander College	USC-Spartanburg
South Carolina State College	USC-Sumter
USC-Aiken	USC-Union
USC-Beaufort	Winthrop College

Source:
South Carolina Commission
on Higher Education
1429 Senate Street
Columbia, South Carolina 29201

During the 1960s and 1970s, when the Christian school movement was experiencing its rapid growth period, the public schools' educational standards were declining. Then it was not difficult for Christian schools to maintain more rigorous standards than the public schools. However, we are now seeing a move back to basic education in the secular schools. They are raising their standards, and many Christian schools are currently seriously deficient. Figures 6.3 and 6.4 illustrate a good typical Christian high-school curriculum with corresponding graduation requirements.

Figure 6.3

Sample Christian High-school Curriculum

Seventh Grade	Eighth Grade	Ninth Grade
Bible	Bible	*Bible
English	English	*English I
Mathematics	Mathematics	*General Math or Algebra I
Geography and / or World History	U.S. History	*Civics, Geography, or State History
Biological Science	Earth Science	*Physical Science
Music/Art	Music/Art	Band or Chorus
		Typing I

Tenth Grade	*Eleventh Grade*	*Twelfth Grade*
*Bible	*Bible	*Bible
*English II	*English III	*English IV
*Geometry or	Algebra II	Advanced Math
Business Math	Computer Science	Computer Science
World History	*U.S. History	*American
		Government
		or Economics
*Biology	Chemistry	Physics
*Physical Education	*Physical Education	*Physical Education
Band or Chorus	Band or Chorus	Band or Chorus
Typing I or II	Typing I or II	
	Shorthand I	Shorthand II
Foreign Language	Foreign Language	

*Required subjects

Figure 6.4

Sample Christian High School Graduation
Requirements

Courses	Units
English	4
Social Studies*	3
Science**	2
Mathematics	2
Health/Physical Education	1
Bible	4
Electives	6
	22

*Includes one unit of U.S. History and one unit of government,
economics, or a combination of the two.
**Includes one unit of biology.

Developing a Master Schedule

Elementary Level

Scheduling for elementary schools is a relatively simple matter. Most conventional schools use self-contained classrooms from kindergarten through the sixth grade, often through the eighth. The four critical considerations mentioned earlier are resolved when a teacher is assigned a specific grade level, classroom, and students, and only minor changes are necessary from year to year. Even when more than one section of a grade is available, scheduling is only slightly more complicated.

It is important, however, that the elementary school day be carefully divided into instructional units. Although teachers' suggestions about these decisions are welcomed by most administrators, the final planning should not be left up to the individual classroom teachers. Schools where the daily schedule is not established by the administration have no assurance that the appropriate amount of time is being allocated for each subject. Inevitably there is a lack of consistency from classroom to classroom. There is no consensus among educators, however, on exactly how a school day should be divided or on what specific subjects must be taught at a particular grade level. These decisions must be based on each school's individual needs. Figure 6.5 can give an idea of a typical first-grade instructional day.

Figure 6.5

Sample Elementary Schedule

Daily Schedule for First Grade

8:00 - 8:15	Homeroom activities
8:15 - 9:00	Bible or Chapel
9:00 - 10:45	Phonics (restroom break at 10:00 - 10:10)
10:45 - 11:00	Reading groups
11:00 - 11:30	Recess
11:30 - 11:45	Reading groups
11:45 - 12:05	Mathematics
12:05 - 12:15	Story time
12:15 - 12:55	Lunch
12:55 - 1:10	Restroom break
1:10 - 2:00	Schedule varies from day-to-day (Art, Mathematics, Heritage Studies, Music, Science, and Physical Education)
2:00 - 2:15	Prepare for dismissal

Because of the need to schedule individual classes for restroom breaks, lunch periods, recess, art, music, and physical education, some differences in class schedules will exist even at the same grade level. But careful scheduling is critical to the smooth operation of a good elementary school.

Secondary Level

Scheduling for the secondary level is more complicated. On the senior-high level, and sometimes on the junior-high level, electives are offered and instruction is departmentalized by academic discipline. Consequently, either teachers or students must move from place to place. Also at this level, the typical school day has from six to nine periods lasting forty-five to sixty minutes. (Occasionally double periods will be needed for special classes.) Some schools schedule no time between classes, while others permit up to ten minutes for changes. Law dictates the length of day in some states, and this may affect the number and length of your class periods. These factors make scheduling more complicated. Figures 6.6 and 6.7 illustrate two sample master schedules.

Figure 6.6
Sample Junior High Master Schedule

	7-1 Homeroom Smith		7-2 Homeroom Collins		7-3 Homeroom James		8-1 Homeroom Mansfield		8-2 Homeroom Helms		8-3 Homeroom Blake	
Homeroom 8:00-8:10	Homeroom Smith	W	Homeroom Collins	X	Homeroom James	Y	Homeroom Mansfield	AA	Homeroom Helms	Z	Homeroom Blake	V
I 8:10-9:00	World History 7 Smith	W	English 7 Collins	W	Life Science 7 James	Y	Earth Science 8 Mansfield	AA	U.S. History 8 Helms	Z	Math 8 Blake	V
II 9:05-9:55	Life Science 7 James	Y	M-Music-Daniels TTh-P.E. WF-Bible-Barnes	Orc Gym X	World History 7 Smith	W	Math 8 Blake	V	Earth Science 8 Mansfield	AA	U.S. History 8 Helms	Z
III 10:00-10:50	English 7 Collins	X	World History 7 Smith	W	Math 7 Mansfield	AA	U.S. History 8 Helms	Z	M-Music-Daniels TTh-P.E. WF-Bible-Wright	Orc Gym V	Earth Science 8 James	Y
11:00-11:40	Junior High Chapel in Assembly Room — MTThF — Student Meetings — W											
11:40-12:50	Lunch											
V 1:00-1:50	Math 7 Blake	V	Math 7 Mansfield	AA	English 7 Collins	X	M-Music-Daniels TTh-P.E. WF-Bible-Wright	Orc Gym Y	English 8 Lewis	Z	MF-Bible-Smith TTh-P.E. W-Music-Daniels	W Gym Orc
VI 1:55-2:45	MF-Bible-Wright TTh-P.E. W-Music-Daniels	AA Gym Orc	Life Science 7 James	Y Y	M-Music-Daniels TTh-P.E. WF-Bible-Rogers	Orc Gym Z	English 8 Smith	W	Math 8 Blake	V	English 8 Collins	X

AFTER-SCHOOL ACTIVITIES

Monday, Wednesday, Friday (3:00-3:40)			Tuesday, Thursday (3:00-4:00)
Band	McGuire	BB	Sports in gymnasium or athletic field
Orchestra	Kline	ORC V	Johns - Girls
Chorus	Daniels		McDonald - Boys

Thursday (4:00-5:00)	
Art Elective	X

54

Figure 6.7

Sample Senior High Master Schedule

Teacher	1 (7:55-8:50)	2 (8:55-9:50)	3 (9:55-10:50)	4 (11:45-12:40)	5 (12:55-1:50)	6 (1:55-2:50)	7 (2:55-3:50)
Adames, Mr.		A German II	A German I		A German I		A English II
Albright, Mr.	G Pre-Algebra	G Pre-Algebra	G Adv. Math		G Algebra II		G Algebra II
Albright, Mrs.					H Geometry	H Geometry	H Geometry
Barnes, Mr.	K MWF Bible II	K TTh Bible IV	K MTTh Bible II		K MTTh Bible II	K TTh Bible IV	K TTh Bible IV
	K TTh Bible IV						
Blake, Mrs.		Lab Dev. Reading	Lab Dev. Reading				
Bridges, Mrs.	PE 9-10 TTh PE 11-12 MWF	PE 11-12 MWF	PE 9-10 WF		PE 9-10 WF	PE 11-12 MWF	PE 11-12 MWF
Craft, Miss		I Algebra I	I Consumer Math		I Algebra I	I Algebra I	I Algebra I
Fields, Mrs.		O Biology	O Biology		O Biology	O Biology	O Biology
Frank, Mr.					Maint. Shop II, III	Maint. Shop I	
Gaines, Miss			BB Girls' Chorus TThF		BB Concert Choir		
Gladen, Mr.	Q MWF Bible I	Q TTh Bible III	Q MTTh Bible I		Z MTTh Bible I	L TTh Bible III	R TTh Bible III
	Q TTh Bible III						
Hoffman, Mr.	D Computer Science	U Physics	T Chemistry		T Chemistry	G Science	
Kipling, Miss		D English I	D English I		D Spanish I	D Spanish II	D Spanish I
Laughton, Miss		R U.S. History	R U.S. History		R U.S. History	R U.S. History	
Lowe, Miss	SL World History	SL World History	SL Amer. Government			SL Amer. Government	
Lund, Mr.	PE 9-10 TTh PE 11-12 MWF	PE 11-12 MWF	PE 9-10 WF		PE 9-10 WF	PE 11-12 MWF	PE 11-12 MWF
Marks, Miss	N English IV	N English IVA			N English IVA	N English IVA	
McCall, Miss	L English III		L English III		L English III		L English III
McEnray, Mr.	S Journalism	S Lettering	S Mechanical Drawing			S Lettering	
Moore, Mr.						E Speech	E Speech
Motley, Mrs.	U Basic Science		U Basic Science			U Basic Science	U Basic Science
Paine, Mrs.		J Typing I	H Shorthand				
Payson, Mrs.		B World Geography	B Economics		B World Geography	Economics	B
Pinkeston, Mr.	Gym Orchestra						
Rose, Miss		C English II	C English II			C English II	
Saven, Mr.	M Driver Education	M Driver Education	M Driver Education	M Driver Education			
Stevens, Mrs.					Lab Study Skills	Lab Study Skills	
Stralow, Mrs.						M English I	M English I
Taylor, Mr.		BB Band					
Tisen, Mrs.					Q Clothing II	Q Foods I	P/Q Foods II
Whitington, Mrs.	J Typing I		J Typing I				

These schedules include the four basic considerations mentioned at the opening of this chapter:

- *Course Requirements:* Be sure that you have considered all the courses necessary for graduation and promotion requirements, and that you have carefully evaluated your school's individual curriculum needs.
- *Teacher Availability:* Course assignments are based on the academic specialization of each faculty member. Consequently, schools plagued with a high turnover may find scheduling more difficult, for as teachers change so do the areas of specialization. Your job is to accommodate these changes and to use a minimum number of teachers to provide required instruction. In scheduling you must also be careful to include lunch periods and preparation periods for each faculty member.
- *Classroom Availability:* With faculty specialization often comes the need for special equipment and sometimes classroom modifications. It may be necessary to reserve one particular room for one specific discipline—a science lab, for example. You will find that in scheduling for the secondary level a classroom chart is a must. These charts may be either purchased from a school supply company or simply made out of cardboard or plywood. An example of a typical layout is illustrated in Figure 6.8.
- *Student Needs:* Having worked out each of the above scheduling problems, you will also need to provide the flexibility in the schedule for individual student needs. For example, students who have failed a course or transferred from other schools may need special scheduling consideration, and all students should be assured access to required courses and electives intended for them. Students should be encouraged to take courses appropriate to their grade level. Those who do not will create serious scheduling difficulties, especially in small schools where only one section of a course is normally offered each year.

Figure 6.8

Classroom Chart

TEACHER										CLASSROOM									
NAME	1	2	3	4	5	6	7	8	9	NUMBER	1	2	3	4	5	6	7	8	9

When the courses have been assigned to teachers and their teaching loads are satisfactory, a schedule board will be helpful in planning your master schedule. The schedule board is an aid in making sure that you have eliminated any conflicts. Figure 6.9 illustrates the layout of the board.

Figure 6.9

Sample Schedule Planning Board

Grade Level	Period 1	Period 2	Period 3	Period 4	Period 5	Period 6	Period 7	Period 8
Nine								
Ten								
Eleven								
Twelve								

We will assume you are going to work with a simple, homemade board. Cut out squares of colored paper a little smaller than the squares on your schedule board. Using different colors, make one square for each teacher for each period of the day. On the squares write the name of each course for each teacher (also the lunch hour, free periods, etc., for each). If you have squares without anything written on them for any teacher, or if you have a course assigned to a teacher that has not yet been written on one of your squares, you have made an error and should recheck your work. When corrections are made, you are ready to proceed with the laying out of the assignments by class periods. Arrange the blocks on the board so that the courses appear on the line for the appropriate grade level. Make sure you have not assigned any teacher to two different courses at the same time. With a little practice you will be able to complete the schedule in a brief time. Room assignments can be handled on a similar schedule board. See Figure 6.10 for a sample board for assigning teachers and classrooms.

Figure 6.10

Sample Board Based on Teachers and Classrooms

Teacher	Period 1	Period 2	Period 3	Period 4	Period 5	Period 6	Period 7	Period 8

Once the master schedule is developed, it should be changed as little as possible from year to year. When changes are necessary, however, they should involve only the time of day courses are offered, and not at what grade level they are offered.

Chapter 6

Other Basic Considerations

Combining Courses

Smaller schools sometimes choose to combine certain lecture classes and offer them in alternate years. This is a good plan if larger classrooms are available. For example, a school might combine some Bible classes. Seventh and eighth grade, ninth and tenth grade, and eleventh and twelfth grade might be combined. This reduces the number of teachers needed and reduces the teachers' preparations. U. S. history and world history could be offered in alternate years and made available to tenth and eleventh graders. Chemistry and physics are also frequently offered in alternate years since enrollments are usually small in upper-level science electives. Scheduling in this way offers definite advantages, but there are some drawbacks. When a course is offered only in alternate years, transfer students can sometimes have difficulty obtaining requirements necessary for graduation.

Overseeing Registration

As counselor you will usually be responsible for student registration. Ideally registration should be completed for old students in the spring. New students can be registered as part of the admissions process. Some schools do not complete their master schedule until the summer; therefore, registration is sometimes delayed until August or even as late as the first day of school. This method is inconvenient for both the student and the school, and it is frequently more costly.

You should have a checksheet for each student similar to the one in Figure 6.11.

Figure 6.11

Student Checksheet

Name _____ Grad. Date _____

Bible ☐ ☐ ☐ ☐   Math ☐☐

                        Algebra ☐☐

English ☐ ☐ ☐ ☐   Econ/Gov't ☐☐

Phy. Ed. ☐☐☐☐   U.S. History ☐

Science ☐☐☐☐   Soc. St. Elect. ☐☐

_____ ☐☐   _____ ☐☐

_____ ☐☐   _____ ☐☐

_____ ☐☐   _____ ☐☐

UNITS   1 2 3 4 5 6 7 8 9 10 11 12 13 14 15 16 17 18 19 20 21 22

This checksheet is based on the curriculum and high school graduation requirements shown in Figures 6.3 and 6.4. It should show all the required courses and have spaces in which elective courses may be written. Different checksheets for the different academic tracks offered by the school are helpful and will tend to minimize errors.

You are responsible to know the student well enough to direct him to the appropriate academic track. Using the record the student has made in school, personal interviews with the student and his parents, and the results of standardized tests, you should have enough information to give sound advice.

It is also wise to involve the parents in the scheduling process. Some schools require the parents to sign the final schedule since, after all, they are paying for their child's education. Students cannot always be relied on to make schedule choices that are in their own best interests. If the student or the parent refuses to schedule according to your advice, the situation should be discussed in a written report that is retained in the student's file for future reference. Of course, the student or the parents would not be permitted to avoid required courses. When dealing only with the student, you should send to the parents a brief informative note similar to the following.

Figure 6.12

Parent's Advisory Letter

Dear Parent:

As you know, it is our policy to encourage each of our students to register for as much academic work as he can reasonably expect to complete satisfactorily. Our evaluation of the student's potential is based on his previous performance both in the classroom and on standardized tests that we have conducted.

Your son John has rejected several suggestions we have made concerning his course selection for next year. We feel that he has avoided courses which he is capable of handling and which may prove to be useful to him if he continues his education beyond high school. He has chosen, instead, general courses that are not recommended for the college-bound student. The final decision on his scheduling is yours, of course, but we want you to know that in our opinion he is capable of more challenging work. By selecting easier courses he is both cheating himself and wasting your valuable dollars for education.

When you have given John's schedule your prayerful consideration, send it back to the school office with your signature. If you would like to discuss the matter with us further, please call the office for an appointment.

Larger schools are now using computers to handle many routine matters such as scheduling. If the school is using a computer for other facets of the administrative or instructional program, it is possible that scheduling could be handled in this way also. However, the expense could probably not be justified for scheduling alone.

Scheduling should be completed far enough in advance of the first day of school for class rolls to be made available to the teachers on the first day. This preparation reassures the students and also contributes greatly to the ability to maintain control of the student body.

7 Spiritual Guidance

Where no counsel is, the people fall: but in the multitude of counsellors there is safety (Prov. 11:14).

Without counsel purposes are disappointed: but in the multitude of counsellors they are established (Prov. 15:22).

For by wise counsel thou shalt make thy war: and in multitude of counsellors there is safety (Prov. 24:6).

The way of a fool is wise in his own eyes: but he that hearkeneth unto counsel is wise (Prov. 12:15).

Many Christian young people are seeking "wise counsel." Unfortunately, such counsel is not always readily available. In their homes, churches, and peer groups they see people who "know" much about Christianity but practice little of what they know. Though there is much said about the joy of the Christian life, the worldly pursuits and desires of many Christians teach young people that Christ is not enough. If there is one message we need to communicate to our students, it is that Christ offers them a better hope than the world. As the Word of God admonishes us, we should "be ready always to give an answer to every man" of the reason of the hope that is in us (I Pet. 3:15). However, it must be a hope that they can recognize as genuine, practical, and alive in our own lives.

As counselors, how can we communicate this message in our ministry? We must first be certain that we have a close personal relationship with our Lord (Eph. 4:14-32; Ps. 24:3-5). When we counsel others, we are attempting to help them return to a right relationship with God. If we are insensitive to sin in our own lives, we cannot hope to guide others, for sin cuts off our communication with God. We can no longer draw from our source of wisdom. Thus we become ineffective. Though God may occasionally use someone who is not right with Him to help another, He does not usually do so.

Second, we must have a thorough knowledge of Scripture (II Tim. 2:15). We need not be theologians to be effective counselors, but it is necessary that we understand basic principles about sin and its consequences. When a believer sins, for example, his offense is first against God (Ps. 51:1-4). To be reconciled to God, he must acknowledge this sin, repent, and seek forgiveness—before taking any further action.

Third, we must also have a sincere desire to be obedient to God's Word. Perfection is not attainable in this life, of course, but every believer should desire perfection (Col. 1:28). As counselors, we cannot resist revealed truth in our own lives and be consistently effective in helping others grow spiritually. Without the working of the Holy Spirit we are powerless, and resisting His leading will make us spiritually weak and undiscerning.

Finally, the counselor must genuinely love people (I John 2:8-11). Scripture commands all Christians to love one another, but the counseling ministry requires special grace. It is difficult to love those who at times scorn our kindnesses and despitefully use us (Matt. 5:44-48). Only the love of Christ flowing through us can make us effective in such circumstances. As counselors, we must submit our personal feelings to the will of God that others may benefit.

Since this is not an entire book on counseling, our treatment of your counseling duties must be as concise as possible. Our purpose in this chapter is to identify some of the problems you will encounter, discuss the way these problems can be solved, and present various methods of counseling.

Identifying the Problems

Several writers have compiled lists of specific problems faced by school counselors. Though the terminology and classifications vary, the problems identified are similar.

In a list of twenty reasons people seek counseling, Adams (1977) includes the following: the need for advice in making simple decisions; the need to find answers to troubling questions; the need for guidance in determining careers; the need for help in dealing with depression and guilt; anxiety, worry, and fear; grief, and other unpleasant feelings; failures; crises; conflicts with others; family conflicts; marital conflicts; deteriorating interpersonal relationships; work difficulties; bizarre behavior; breakdowns;

sexual difficulties; perceptual distortions; psychosomatic problems; and suicide attempts.

Meier, Minirth, and Wichern (1982) compiled a list of the following ten problem areas: anxiety, fear, self-control, irritability, lust, depression, guilt, worry, guidance, and lack of confidence.

Similar lists have been prepared by other writers. As we examine these various problem areas, however, one truth becomes clear— though times change, people do not. "The thing that hath been, it is that which shall be; and that which is done is that which shall be done: and there is no new thing under the sun" (Eccles. 1:9).

Solving the Problems

Realizing that man has not changed is the first prerequisite to solving any problem. Man's basic problem is rebellion against God (I Sam. 15:22-26). We tend to disregard the fact that man had no problems until the fall. Sin entered the world through man's disobedience (Gen. 3:17), and rebellion continues to be the center of his problems. At the risk of being simplistic, a list of basic principles follows in Figure 7.1.

Figure 7.1
Basic Principles of Counseling

1. Every problem is a spiritual problem and, therefore, has a biblical solution (I Cor. 10:13; Heb. 4:15).
2. Everyone is responsible for his actions, regardless of the circumstances (II Cor. 5:10; Heb. 9:27).
3. The real counselor is the Holy Spirit. The human counselor, aside from what God has done for him and will do through him, has nothing to offer those in trouble (Isa. 9:6; John 14:16-17; Gal. 3:1,3).
4. All counseling should be based on the Word of God (John 17:8, 14-17).
5. Christian counseling must be directive. God has a will for every person and a solution to every problem. The job of the counselor is to help the troubled student come to genuine peace with God by developing a right relationship with Him. Then, the counselor should assist him in finding God's will for his life (Prov. 2; John 14:26).
6. The counselor must help the student depend directly on the Holy Spirit to guide him (I John 2:27).

This list is not comprehensive, nor do we suggest that you can resolve all problems by carefully applying these principles. We do believe, however, that as a beginning counselor you will be amazed at the broad applications that can be made from these few points.

One of your first duties in counseling students will be to help the student identify his sin and acknowledge his responsibility for it, and seek forgiveness and restoration. Anything less is like giving aspirin for a fever; it may alleviate the symptoms, but it fails to cure the root cause.

We must also help the students realize that unconfessed sin has a continuing destructive influence in their lives. We like to believe that by ignoring problems they will go away, but we must realize that unconfessed sin will not disappear; it will lead to more sin. David's sin with Bathsheba (II Sam. 11) vividly illustrates this truth. David's refusal to acknowledge his sin of adultery drove him to lie, to tempt others to sin, and eventually to murder Uriah. The results of this tragedy were God's judgment on David personally and suffering for other family members.

At times we may counsel students who are having to deal with a problem initiated by the sinful behavior of someone else. In this case we must help them recognize that God is interested in their response to Him through this circumstance. Though they are not accountable for the other person's behavior, they are accountable for how they react to the situation. God's dealing with Abraham (Gen. 22) may be a good example to use. When God commanded Abraham to sacrifice Isaac, Abraham did not know that Isaac's life would be spared. He did not fully understand the circumstances, but he obeyed the command (Heb. 11:17-19). This obedient reaction confirmed his love for God above all else, and God rewarded this love. At times our testing will stop just short of the sacrifice, as in Abraham's case. At other times we may be called on to complete the sacrifice. In either case we must trust God and obey His commands.

The counselor's approach will be based on what he believes; thus, as a Christian counselor you must base your approach on the Word of God. Identifying specific passages that apply to specific problems will prove invaluable. The student must see the direct association between the solution to his problem and Scripture. If he does not clearly see this connection, his confidence may rest in you rather than the Lord. This specific approach will also help you to remember that it is God's Word, not your explanation, that He chooses to bless. Appendix E at the end of the book may be helpful to you as you begin your study.

A follow-up program can be a valuable means of providing spiritual counsel to students even after they have left school. Though most administrators agree that such a program is important, few Christian schools have a formal system of surveying graduates and dropouts. Following up former students is a great opportunity for Christian schools. Few former students object to being contacted by their school if they are convinced that the outreach is a genuine expression of Christian love. If former students have specific spiritual needs, a follow-up program could provide the opportunity to meet those needs. If, on the other hand, they are using their training for the Lord, a contact would encourage them to provide prayer and possibly financial support for the school. In any case, your outreach is extended.

It may be helpful to mention here that in this realm of spiritual counseling it is best if the counselor is of the same sex as the student. In working with younger children, kindergarten through sixth grade, the sex of the counselor is not usually significant. From the junior high school upward, however, it is easier for the counselor to develop a good rapport if he is of the same sex as the student he is counseling. This consideration is especially important on the high school level. Ideally the school should have two counselors, a man and a woman. If the school is small, however, this may not be feasible. As an alternative a teacher of the opposite sex of the counselor could be trained to assist in counseling duties.

One other consideration bears mentioning. In some schools the counselor may also be given the responsibility of discipline. This approach is not recommended. It is difficult to serve as both judge and counselor. It is easier to have an effective restoration ministry through counseling if the administration of discipline and the role of counseling can be handled by different people.

Using Appropriate Methods

There are two common methods of counseling— directive and nondirective. Since Carl Rogers, counseling including Christian counseling, has become more nondirective. But which method is biblical? Is it a matter of the counselor's choice? Let's examine both methods before giving a definite answer.

In the directive method the counselor attempts to help the troubled person identify his problem and then directs him to a specific solution to the problem. The nondirective counselor, however, attempts to help the person discern his problem and encourages him to select a solution that seems appropriate and satisfactory to him. In other words, a nondirective counselor would never tell a person whether his behavior was good or bad or that his proposed solution was right or wrong. The nondirective counselor believes that when an individual has the opportunity to discuss his problem, he will inevitably come to a solution best for him in the given circumstances.

Of course, there are degrees of directive and nondirective counseling. There is the nondirective counselor who keeps those with whom he works barely afloat, letting them swim in any direction they choose. There are others who structure the choices in such a way that they hope the counselee will make the right choice. On the other hand, there are directive counselors who are so narrow that the counselee is forced to fit into precise molds deemed right by the counselor himself.

Considering the goals and purposes of Christian counseling, it is evident that extremes are not acceptable. It is important to realize, however, that the nondirective approach is never valid for Christian counseling. The Christian counselor must help the person identify his specific spiritual problem and then direct him to the specific biblical solution. These goals cannot be achieved by the nondirective method. The directive approach, however, will lead him to the specific biblical solution to that problem. The directive approach enables the counselor to rely on Scripture as the absolute standard by which to measure all behavior. In nondirective counseling there are no such absolutes, for truth is relative and will change with each changing circumstance. Unfortunately, some Christian counselors do try to use this approach. It is evident, however, that by doing so they undermine their entire ministry.

We believe that the Bible is the Word of God. It does not contain harmful ambiguities. Within its pages are found answers to every problem, hope for every sinner, and direction for all who walk with Him. Man cannot mend his relationship with God through his own "solutions." He must rather approach God, acknowledge his sin and seek forgiveness. The Christian counselor has a responsibility to those he seeks to help; he must lead them to understand God's expectations for them.

A final observation about spiritual counseling may be helpful. We should remember that regardless of our experience we will encounter problems from time to time that are beyond the scope of our ability. Obviously this will occur more frequently in the early stages of our counseling career. It is important that we acknowledge any situation that we cannot deal with, and we should refer the person in need to someone who is equipped to help him. This is especially important when the counselee is seriously disturbed, suicidal, apparently under demonic influence, or possibly suffering from serious physical problems.

Chapter 7

The good counselor never loses sight of the fact that he is only God's instrument. It is the Holy Spirit who is responsible for the victories in the lives of those needing our help. We must be careful not to take credit that belongs to the Lord. As soon as possible, we should encourage the counselee to seek help directly from God. From the beginning our duty is to work ourselves out of a job.

8 Appraisal of Students

Student appraisal involves the development of a wide range of significant information. The purposes of pupil appraisal are to develop an accurate description of each student; to use this information to guide him spiritually; and to direct him in making appropriate educational decisions, both academic and vocational. As counselor you play an important role in collecting, maintaining, and communicating this necessary information.

Large schools that have several full-time counselors with secretarial support frequently have elaborate and extensive appraisal systems. Although these programs may develop much useful information, they are more time-consuming and demanding than the small Christian school can manage. Recognizing this fact, this chapter emphasizes appraisal techniques and materials that are most useful to small- to medium-sized schools. Larger schools can easily adapt these suggestions to meet their own needs. We will first list the information that all schools should maintain in each student's file each year; then, we will discuss the two methods used to obtain this information.

- A record of the subjects taken and the grade received
- An evaluation of the student's behavior
- A record of attendance
- The results of all standardized achievement and mental ability testing, including the name of the tests and the dates the tests were administered
- Anecdotal reports
- Observation reports
- At the secondary level, a record of the student's involvement in extracurricular activities
- A list of any special achievements or awards and the date received
- Health records (certificates of immunization and copy of birth certificate should be included)

The methods of obtaining the student appraisal information fall into two categories: the nonstandardized and the standardized methods.

Nonstandardized Methods

Evaluation of Academic Progress

As counselor, you are responsible for monitoring the academic progress of each student. Your role in grading is usually to standardize procedures for collecting grades, to complete report cards, to distribute report cards, to record grade information on student records, and to make certain that a uniform and equitable grading system is followed. These duties involve not only careful organization but also much paperwork. It is preferable, therefore, that you have clerical assistance once the school is large enough to provide such help. You will then be free to spend more of your time collecting and distributing this valuable information to those needing it.

Evaluation of Behavior

You can also assist in collecting behavioral data and in making sure that the methods for obtaining this data are consistent school-wide or at least within specific grade levels. Generally, the classroom teachers evaluate the behavior of all students for each grading period, at least through grade six. Some schools continue to evaluate behavior through grade twelve by using either teacher's reports or a demerit system. Where conduct grades are given, either the traditional letter grades may be used or a special grading scale may be adopted. The most important thing is that the marking system be easily understood, for it must be understood to be helpful.

Another important source of information is observation of students by the professional staff. Though this source is informal and highly subjective, it is valuable. Two ways of recording these observations is through anecdotal or general observation reports. Since some students may go through several years of school without being involved in any activities that would merit an anecdotal report, like the one in Figure 8.1, general observation reports are necessary. (See Figure 8.2.)

Figure 8.1

Anecdotal Report

Student Name _____ Observed by _____

Where observed _____

When observed (date) _____ (time) _____

Description of incident observed:

Action taken, response of student, additional comments:

Figure 8.2

Observation Report

Student Name _____ Academic Year _____

Grade Level (K 1 2 3 4 5 6 7 8 9 10 11 12) circle one

Instructions: At least annually all teachers must complete an Observation Report on each student they teach. This report should be based on the teacher's personal experience with a student, not what has been reported by others. The report should cover observations made for this academic year only, with an emphasis on the behavior as of the end of the year. Special note should be made if the student was evaluated prior to checking out for the end of the year.

Place a checkmark before each item you believe to be representative of this student.

Positive Traits	Negative Traits
____ 1. professes to be saved	____ 1. admits to being unsaved
____ 2. shows interest in spiritual things	____ 2. appears to be unsaved
____ 3. is spiritually mature for age	____ 3. resists spiritual direction
____ 4. exerts above average effort to achieve	____ 4. exerts less than average effort to achieve
____ 5. exerts average effort to achieve	____ 5. dislikes school
____ 6. is neat in appearance	____ 6. has unkempt appearance
____ 7. is in good health	____ 7. has poor attendance record
____ 8. is polite	____ 8. is unreliable
____ 9. is considerate	____ 9. is uncooperative
____ 10. is well liked	____ 10. is rude
____ 11. is creative	____ 11. has questionable integrity
____ 12. demonstrates initiative	____ 12. is too aggressive
____ 13. is prompt	____ 13. seems insecure
____ 14. is a good leader	____ 14. resists authority
____ 15. accepts responsibility	____ 15. is unwilling to accept responsibility

Additional comments:

Evaluated by:

Date:

_____

School supply firms have standard forms available both for anecdotal and observation reports; however, most Christian schools will want to design their own forms to incorporate spiritual insights. You will find that if you provide forms like the ones illustrated, your teachers will more readily record their observations for school use.

The specific observations you as the counselor make during personal student interviews may also prove beneficial. Figure 8.3 illustrates a form that may be used in conducting these interviews. It would be profitable to have a program of personal interviews for students in grades seven and above on an annual basis. The data developed could be used in counseling and in making re-enrollment decisions.

Figure 8.3

Spiritual Inventory: Counselor's Report

Date of Annual Interview _____ Counselor _____

Student's Name _____ Grade _____ School Year _____

Spiritual Condition:

If student professes to be saved, give a summary of his salvation experience:

_____

_____

_____

_____

_____

List verses student uses to substantiate his salvation experience: _____

_____ Can he quote them? _____

Evidence of Obedience:

Describe student's attitude toward baptism, church attendance, and church membership: _____

_____

Describe student's devotional activities: _____

_____

Describe the student's plans for the future. What indication if any is there that the student has definitely sought God's will for his future? _____

_____

_____

_____

_____

Does the student plan to go on to college or other formal education? Yes ____

No ____ If yes, where does the student plan to go, what type of training is to be pursued? _____

_____

A self-report inventory also provides a source of helpful information. Figure 8.4 shows a form designed to be used in this way. However, students cannot always be relied on to provide an accurate evaluation of themselves. But, generally, a review of the overall content of the inventory will show whether the student is responding honestly.

Figure 8.4

Spiritual Inventory: Student's Self-report

Name _____ Grade _____ School Year _____

Answer the following questions as honestly as you can.

To the best of my personal knowledge I am:

Saved _____ Unsaved _____ Uncertain _____

Walking closely to the Lord _____ Am not as close to the Lord as I should be or have been in the past _____

Participation in spiritual activities:

I attend Sunday School
               regularly _____ occasionally _____ seldom_____

I attend worship services
               regularly _____ occasionally _____ seldom_____

I attend prayer meeting
               regularly _____ occasionally _____ seldom_____

I participate in youth activities
               regularly _____ occasionally _____ seldom_____

Personal life:

I read my Bible daily   Yes _____ No _____

I pray daily   Yes _____ No _____

I memorize Scripture   Yes _____ No _____

I witness to lost people   Yes _____ No _____

Quality of personal relationships:

What kind of relationship do you have with the following people:

Father   good _____ average _____ poor _____

Mother   good _____ average _____ poor _____

Brothers/Sisters   good _____ average _____ poor _____

Other family members   good _____ average _____ poor _____

How would you describe
  your family life?   good _____ average _____ poor _____

If you could go to school anywhere you wanted to, where would you go?

Record of Participation in Extracurricular Activities

This information should be routinely kept as part of the permanent record; however, such information may be useful in appraising students. Participation or lack of participation may, together with other available information, provide valuable insight into a student's personality.

Special Awards

Closely related to extracurricular activities is the record of special awards. This record may include the honor roll, any other academic recognition, scholarships, perfect attendance, citizenship awards, athletic accomplishments, and anything not given to all the participants in any school-sponsored or other recognized activity. This record may be as brief or as detailed as the school administrators wish.

Standardized Tests

Any honest consideration of standardized testing must include some thought about the criticism of testing developed in recent years. Testing has been abused at times by those whose understanding of the method is limited or erroneous. Some students have been incorrectly labeled as a result of testing, and their lives, consequently, negatively influenced. Shertzer and Stone (1981) have listed ten general criticisms of tests and testing:

1. Mental ability test scores often result in the categorization of students early in life; such classification limits their success and status in life.
2. Standardized tests have been the object of serious criticism concerning reliability and validity.
3. Standardized tests are not free of racial, social, and cultural bias.
4. Standardized tests place considerable emphasis on verbal and quantitative skills that are not reflective of all types of achievement in our society.
5. Standardized testing of necessity invades the privacy of the student.
6. The results of testing are frequently not made available to the student, his parents, and sometimes not even his teachers.
7. The producers of standardized tests, rather than professional educators in the schools, control the curriculum.
8. Frequent testing encourages the student to develop test-taking skills without real learning.

9. Standardized testing encourages a tendency toward mechanistic decision making.
10. Standardized testing results in an inappropriate emphasis on individual competition.

To a degree, there is justification for each of these criticisms. But the primary problem with standardized testing is not the above criticisms but rather the indiscreet or unwise use of the data obtained from the tests. Despite this weakness, however, standardized tests are worthwhile. They, in fact, measure knowledge and factual information better than any other currently available method. Two worthwhile pamphlets on the proper use of standardized testing have been written by Robert L. Ebel (1977) and Vito Perrone (1977). These pamphlets are entitled *The Uses of Standardized Testing* and *The Abuses of Standardized Testing*. This material should be part of every Christian school's professional library.

In recent years state, regional, and national Christian school associations have been interested in developing a broad range of testing programs. Some groups have been successful in getting widespread support within their organizations. This interest is profitable. It will make it possible to develop useful norms within the Christian school movement. These norms will not only aid individual schools in evaluating their students and faculty but also give them a basis of comparison with other public and private schools. Cooperative efforts for testing can also be economical.

Christian school associations desiring to develop testing programs would be wise to consider incorporating both achievement and mental ability testing. This combination will enable the individual school to effectively compare student performance with student ability, the most valuable form of comparison.

The five types of standardized tests most frequently recommended for schools are the following: mental ability, aptitude, academic achievement, personality, and interest. Most educators agree that educationally, mental ability and achievement tests are essential. Aptitude and interest tests are also useful for the Christian school. However, personality tests, are highly suspect. Though we will briefly examine each of these tests, a list of test publishers is included in Appendix F. If you want to review the materials currently available, a description of the tests may be obtained by writing directly to those publishers.

Mental Ability Tests
The intended purpose of mental ability testing is to provide an overall measure of general ability, particularly the student's

facility for mastering school-related tasks. Though the object of considerable criticism, mental ability test scores are useful when their limitations are understood. As is true of any standardized test, they are most valuable when considered in conjunction with other academic data. Mental ability tests fall into two categories: individual tests and group tests. Since special training is usually required to administer and interpret the results of individual tests, schools normally use group tests.

Some of the more common group mental ability tests are the Cognitive Abilities Test, the Otis-Lennon Mental Ability Test, and the Test of Cognitive Skills.

Aptitude Tests

Aptitude and intelligence are frequently used interchangeably, but important, subtle differences exist between the two terms. Intelligence refers to general levels of ability, whereas aptitude refers to more specific levels of ability.

The purpose of aptitude testing is to identify the student's potential abilities. This information is useful in providing educational and vocational direction and in making certain predictions about success in specific academic or vocational areas.

Two examples of commonly used aptitudes tests are the American College Test (ACT) and the Scholastic Aptitude Test (SAT).

Academic Achievement Tests

Achievement tests are perhaps the most common form of standardized tests used by schools. Both the reliability and validity of nationally standardized tests have been well established. These tests are designed to measure academic learning in specific areas of curriculum. Therefore, if the test measures the academic content taught in your school, the test results are valid and may by used to evaluate the students' progress and the teachers' effectiveness.

Among the most frequently used tests are the California Achievement Tests, Comprehensive Test of Basic Skills, Iowa Test of Basic Skills, the Test of Achievement and Proficiency, the Metropolitan Achievement Tests, the Science Research Associates Achievement Tests, the Stanford Achievement Tests, and the Stanford Test of Academic Skills.

Personality Tests

The purpose of personality testing is to help the individual better understand himself. Personality tests come in a variety of forms. Some are simple self-administered tests. Others are more complex. However, all reflect humanistic assumptions about personality. Consequently, they are not recommended for general Christian school use. They are not likely to be helpful and may possibly be harmful.

Interest Tests

Expressions of student interest are especially helpful to you in career counseling. Simple ranking by the students of various vocations in the order of greatest to least interest to him may be profitable. Standardized measures of interest can be of much greater help. However, the results of these tests are oriented toward a secular view of employment. The results must, therefore, be interpreted with this limitation in mind.

Among the more common standardized interest inventories in current use are the Kuder Preference Record, the Strong-Campbell Interest Inventories, the Ohio Vocational Interest Survey, and the Career Maturity Inventory.

Developing a Standardized Testing Program

Implementing Testing Procedures

Let's look further at the standardized achievement and mental ability tests. The other areas require little or no special funding and can be handled with a reasonable level of cooperation and support from the classroom teachers and the administration. However, a standardized testing program requires substantial funding that is not always readily available. Standardized testing for achievement and mental ability may run as much as two dollars per student tested and will, therefore, cost the school several hundred dollars annually. Few administrators will make such an investment unless they believe the results will be valuable.

We must first understand what constitutes a minimally acceptable program. We defined an acceptable testing program for new students in Chapter 5. Ideally, all students should have achievement tests annually. If not tested each year, the students should be tested at least periodically. The varying levels and forms of the test will diminish the possibility of the students becoming too familiar with the tests.

Unfortunately, many school officials do not feel that they can justify the expense of this important program. An acceptable alternative is to administer academic achievement tests at specified grade levels. For example, all students could be tested in the first, fourth, eighth, and eleventh grades. Seniors should also be required to take either the American College Test (ACT) or the Scholastic

Aptitude Test (SAT), the two most frequently used college admissions tests.

Mental ability tests should also be administered to students in first, fourth, eighth, and eleventh grades. More frequent administration of this test would not be worthwhile. If, however, the accuracy of the test results are questioned for a specific student, you may want to give a different mental ability test in order to compare the scores.

Most test publishers provide scoring assistance and peel-off labels that can be attached to each student's permanent record folders. The cost of these services is minimal considering the time and expense involved in scoring and posting. Credibility also increases when tests are scored by an outside agency in much the same way that credibility is enhanced when a financial audit is performed by an independent CPA firm.

Using Test Results

Once a standardized testing program has been implemented, what should be done with the test results? Ironically, some schools go to the trouble of implementing a program and administering the tests and then do nothing with the results. The information is not shared with the students, parents, or faculty members. This is obviously a waste of time and money. Using test results effectively, however, requires understanding of some basic testing and measurement principles.

Standardized tests are not absolute measures of anything. They reflect what the student is able to recall and is willing to share at any given point about the subject being evaluated. Unfortunately, if the student is ill, does not understand the questions, is confused about the test format, or does not see the relevance of the test, his scores may be seriously distorted. Obviously, under such circumstances those seeking to evaluate the student do not get an accurate picture of his ability.

The test results may also reflect a degree of imperfection in the test design. Were the questions about the subject relevant? Did they reflect what every student should at the time be expected to know about the subject? It is important that we consider the educational philosophy of the test writer if we are to measure the value of the test's content. If the test does not measure the content we consider important, then the results will be unsatisfactory.

As mentioned in Chapter 5, most standardized test scores are expressed in terms of grade equivalent, stanines, percentiles, and standard scores. Grade equivalent scores are an attempt to express performance in terms of average scores made by students in a particular grade. Stanine scores are a means of expressing scores on a scale of 1-9. Percentiles are expressed on a scale of 1-99 with a median of 50. Standard scores convert individual raw scores by the following formula:

$$\frac{\text{X (raw score)} - \text{M (mean)}}{\text{SD (standard deviation)}}$$

The ACT and SAT report standard scores. More detailed explanations of the scores are included in introductory materials accompanying the tests.

Of all the scores recorded, perhaps the easiest for the untrained individual to understand are percentiles. An individual's score represents his relative performance compared to others taking the test. If a student's score is equal to or greater than 60 percent of the other students, we say that score is at the 60th percentile. For illustration we will use percentiles, although similar comparisons could be made with other scores. One thing that must be remembered in working with percentiles is that they should not be used to develop a mean (arithmetic average). The median (middle score) should be used in averaging. This can be done by simply ranking all scores in the order of highest to lowest and identifying the middle one.

Once tests have been administered and scored, it is helpful to develop charts to picture how the school, and various components within the school, have performed. The charts make comparison of individual scores with others within the school easier. It also makes possible comparison between schools and classes within the school with the national norms. Figures 8.5, 8.6, and 8.7 are examples of how scores may be examined.

Figure 8.5

Median Achievement/Mental Ability of
All Students Enrolled in Grades 1-5

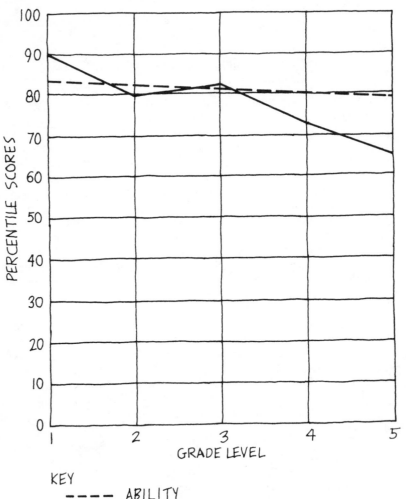

KEY
- - - - ABILITY
———— ACHIEVEMENT

MEDIAN ABILITY OF STUDENTS ENROLLED
IN GRADES ONE THROUGH FIVE — 81%
MEDIAN ACHIEVEMENT OF STUDENTS ENROLLED
IN GRADES ONE THROUGH FIVE — 81%

Figure 8.6

Median Achievement/Mental Ability of
All Students Enrolled in Grades 6-9

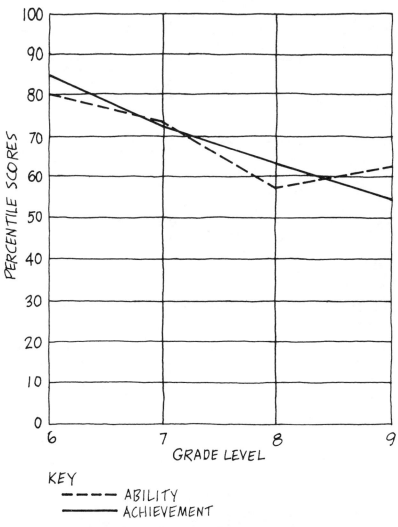

KEY

– – – – ABILITY

———— ACHIEVEMENT

MEDIAN ABILITY OF STUDENTS ENROLLED
IN GRADES SIX THROUGH NINE – 73%

MEDIAN ACHIEVEMENT OF STUDENTS ENROLLED
IN GRADES SIX THROUGH NINE – 75%

Figure 8.7

Achievement/Mental Ability of One
Student as Reflected by Standardized
Test Scores in Grades 1-9

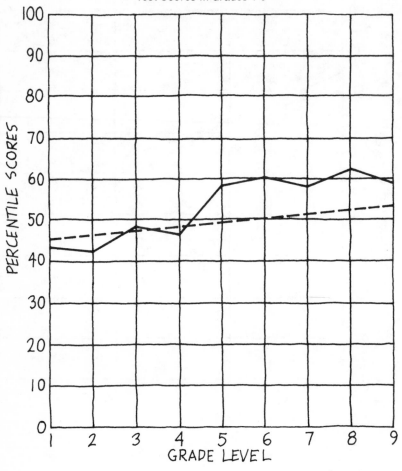

KEY

– – – – ABILITY
———— ACHIEVEMENT

MEDIAN ABILITY AS TESTED IN
GRADES ONE, FOUR, AND EIGHT – 48%
MEDIAN ACHIEVEMENT AS TESTED IN
GRADES ONE THROUGH NINE – 58%

Most achievement tests give a composite score for the entire test. This score represents an overall average of achievement measured by the examination. It is an important score. Perhaps more important in helping students, however, is the individual score given for the specific subjects. For example, scores in reading, mathematics, science, or social studies enable the teacher to identify specific strengths and weaknesses of individual students.

Theoretically, there is no limit to the types of comparisons that could be made based on the scores earned on standardized academic achievement and mental ability tests. For comparison, it is suggested that you consider the following as a minimum:

1. Determine the median percentile composite score for academic achievement for the entire school and for each grade level.
2. Determine the median percentile score on the mental ability test for the entire school and for each grade level. Where more than one score is available, use either the more recent score or the average of all the scores available.
3. Determine the median percentile for each subject at each grade level.

For a more in-depth discussion of the use of testing and the interpretation of test scores, we suggest that you consult a specialized text.

Whatever achievement levels of the school are examined as a means of measuring the effectiveness of the overall academic program, those levels must be viewed in conjunction with a review of the ability level of the students. The ability level of the student is illustrated in Figure 8.7. The median percentile of the student represented is in the 48th percentile. The median achievement percentile for the school is in the 58th percentile. The achievement level is somewhat above what would be expected. Consequently, we can assume that there is an effective academic program. This knowledge of the ability level and achievement level of students is useful in reaching a wide range of decisions in the schools.

Making decisions about students based on the information discussed in this chapter is not an exact science. Decisions made involve important assumptions that must be clearly understood. These decisions assume that the grades given by teachers are objective and accurate. They assume that anecdotal records and observation reports are reasonably free of personal bias. They assume that the specific standardized test given in the school reflects the instruction received in the school. Though any one or all of these factors may be somewhat tainted, the collective information represents the basis for far more intelligent decisions than their only alternative—an uneducated guess.

9 Academic Guidance

As we have seen, your administrative and clerical duties give you the opportunity to evaluate student potential and progress carefully. You are, therefore, in a position to use this information to aid the student by realistically determining his potential and by encouraging him to exercise his God given abilities in service.

Maintaining A Biblical Perspective

Every person is uniquely different in appearance, capabilities, and opportunities (I Cor. 4:7, 12:4, and Matt. 25:15). Likewise, our relationship to God is individual. We are saved by a personal faith in Christ, and we are specifically called to serve Him. He equips us for service and enables us to fulfill successfully our responsibilities through His grace (Exod. 4:10-12, Prov. 2:3-5, Eccles. 2:26, Dan. 1:15-20, Luke 21:15, Phil. 1:6, 4:19, James 1:5, and II Pet. 3:9).

God's expectations of us are in accordance with the gifts and opportunities He has given us. Each of us needs to be careful to use the opportunities He provides to develop our talents (Matt. 25:24-29, Mic. 6:8). God will not hold us accountable for what He has given to another. He will evaluate us individually, not on the basis of how impressive our service appears, but on the basis of how fully we have developed our personal abilities and how completely we have yielded these abilities to Him (Mark 12:41-44 and Col. 3:22-24). These principles are extremely important for school personnel to understand, for if we are to be successful in training our students to serve the Lord our perspective must be right.

Determining Individual Potential

Though as Christian educators we emphasize academic excellence, we do not make academic achievement an end in itself. The goal of all Christian education is the development of Christ-like character in students. The academic training we provide is designed to prepare the student for God's use, and our academic counseling is a means of directing the student into an appropriate place of service. But in order to give wise academic counsel, we must understand and accept the differences in individual learning potential.

As mentioned in Chapter 8, standardized achievement tests, mental ability tests, and grades are some of the tools that can be valuable in helping us discern individual potential. There are, however, other common assumptions about measuring intelligence and evaluating learning with which you as counselor ought to be familiar. As you will see by the following discussion, some of these assumptions are valid, but others are not.

One explanation for differences in academic achievement is that some people are innately more intelligent than others. It is thus assumed that if we can test innate intelligence, we can predict future academic success. This assumption, of course, has some validity. However, we must remember that testing is a limited evaluative tool. First, no test has been developed which can precisely measure innate intelligence. Furthermore, few people ever perform up to 100 percent of their potential. Consequently, tests of mental ability can precisely predict future academic achievement only if the scores obtained reflect a realistic estimation of the individual's ability and if the individual will continue to exert the same amount of effort in the future. In other words, though these tests are useful, they are not infallible and must be used along with other evaluative tools.

A second theory states that most people are essentially equal in innate learning ability, but they develop individual levels of motivation and skills necessary for academic achievement. These motivational and skill factors account for the wide variation in student achievement. Those who hold this view believe that most people are capable of learning even complex and abstract skills, if they are motivated to learn what is presented. Though we do not agree that people possess equal abilities, it does appear that most people have sufficient innate ability to learn those skills necessary to function effectively in society.

Some people contend that those from certain racial and ethnic backgrounds have different levels of intelligence based on genetic inheritance. Research has shown that this view is erroneous.

Some educators suggest that intelligence is a fixed quantity that never changes, but numerous studies have offered evidence to counter this view. Although it is likely that a person's potential is fixed by God at conception, certain conditions can prevent him from realizing this potential. Physical abuse through the consumption of alcohol, tobacco, and other drugs can cause temporary or even permanent mental damage. Disease and illness can also affect mental capacity. On the other hand, by improving his test-taking ability, an individual may appear more intelligent at one time than another. Of course, God also can supernaturally intervene and enable an individual to perform beyond his normal capabilities.

While intelligence refers to the capacity to learn, learning means the development, application, or use of this capacity. Of those factors consistently related to student achievement, few are within the power of the school and its personnel to change. Research confirms that students with equal ability achieve according to the effort they expend. Most of what students learn in their academic subjects results from their deliberate, intentional actions. This is not to say that a mere decision to learn will automatically insure a mastery of the material, but unless a student decides to learn a given task there is virtually no chance of his doing so. Experienced teachers know that learning requires a cooperative student. Thus, if we wish to increase academic achievement, we will make the greatest progress by concentrating on strategies that encourage maximum student effort.

Encouraging Individual Achievement

As Christian educators, we are concerned with placing the student in contact with information and experiences that will initiate spiritually positive changes in his behavior. The nature of intelligence and its relationship to learning have been studied closely over the years. Our further discussion of this subject is based on the assumption that all students accepted into your school program have at least the minimum ability required to perform successfully your school-related tasks, if they can be motivated to exert a reasonable effort. Figure 9.1 lists several factors that affect student achievement.

Figure 9.1

Factors Affecting Achievement

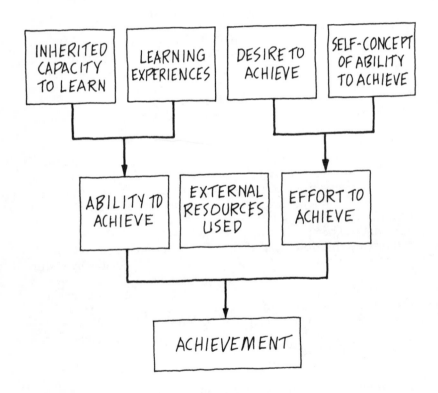

Source:
From "Schooling and Learning—The Principal's Influence on Student Achievement" by K. M. Matthews and C. L. Brown, *NASSP Bulletin,* 60, p. 9.

Traditionally, when we speak of learning, we think of the acquisition of new skills such as spelling, writing, and mathematics. Learning, of course, encompasses more than these specific areas. It also involves the development of motor skills, memorization skills, and reasoning skills. Students likewise develop a system of values in school. Unfortunately, they may at this time also learn negative behavioral patterns such as stuttering, flinching, withdrawing, fantasizing, or belligerence. Obviously, students learn far more in school than what is recorded on a report card.

As educators we must recognize that we can either help improve or retard our students' learning. The remainder of this chapter will be devoted to discussing not only the impact we as educators can have but also the impact parents, relatives, and peers have on student performance.

A student expecting success in a particular venture is more likely to carry through than is the student who fears failure or undesirable results. Educators agree that anticipation of the outcome is a greater determining factor in achievement than even the intense desire to master a certain behavior (Brookover & Erickson, 1975, p. 270).

Research also shows that self-concept of ability is more positively and consistently linked to academic achievement than any other single factor. Wilbur Brookover, one of the nation's leading researchers on self-concept of ability and achievement, defines self-concept of ability as the individual's assessment of his competency to carry out the behavior appropriate for the role. This assessment functions as a threshold variable. In other words, an individual must assume some probability of at least minimal success before he will attempt a given task (Brookover & Erickson, 1975, p. 275). Though some people with high self-concept of abilities are low achievers, those who are consistently high achievers always believe that they can be high achievers. For this reason we refer to self-concept of ability as a threshold condition. An individual will inevitably first perform the task mentally and evaluate the results before deciding whether the results are worth the effort.

Initially, self-concept was viewed as a somewhat universal perception for an individual. Further research, however, showed that self-concept can vary from general self-worth to self-concept of ability in a specific academic discipline. It has also been discovered that self-concept may vary from day to day and even within a day depending on the stimuli at work on the individual. Generally, self-concepts are stable, as are other behavioral patterns, and once observed, can be counted on to be repeated unless some specific intervention precipitates a change in a person's self-perception. The longer a self-concept is held, the more permanent it is. We must understand that the self-concept does not have to be based on truth. A student's perception of himself may be totally false; nonetheless, he will make decisions based on this false perception. If failure results, he will be reluctant to attempt a similar task regardless of the fact that he may be innately capable of successful performance (Purkey, 1970).

These assumptions, erroneous or not, provide a frame of reference for future decision-making. James Coleman noted that an individual's frame of reference can be classified into three categories: assumptions about fact, value, and possibility (1960, p. 58). Expressed another way, every individual bases his behavior on how he thinks things really are, how he thinks things should be, or how he thinks things could be. A wealth of research is available supporting the significant correlation of self-concept of ability and academic performance. The studies have involved students in most parts of the world at all levels of formal education and have included both normal and exceptional children, those whose behavior was socially acceptable, and those whose behavior was not. The relationship between self-concept of academic ability and achievement at all levels of education has been well established (Brookover & Erickson, 1975).

Since self-concept of ability plays such a powerful role in determining student achievement, it is imperative that Christian educators understand what factors determine self-concept.

There is a group of people in the life of every person that we will refer to as "significant others." These people can greatly affect self-concept. For school-age young people, this group comprises parents, brothers and sisters, other relatives, friends, neighbors, and teachers. Figure 9.2 and 9.3 illustrate how 561 students viewed the influence of significant others in respect to their academic success. It is worth noting that teachers come second only to parents in the strength of their influence. It is also interesting to note the relative unimportance of peer groups.

Figure 9.2

General Influence of "Significant Others"

Percentage of the Same Students at Each Grade Level Who Name at Least One Person in Each of the Following Categories of Significant Others as Being *Important in Their Lives*
(Males = 255 and Females = 306)

Categories of Others		Grade 8	Grade 9	Grade 10	Grade 11	Grade 12
General "Significant Others"	*Sex*	%	%	%	%	%
Parent (s)	M	97	96	96	95	93
	F	99	98	96	98	98
Age Level Relatives	M	62	60	46	52	57
	F	76	75	70	78	75
Adult Relatives	M	38	40	27	35	31
	F	55	57	47	53	52
Friends, Same Sex	M	44	48	26	33	27
	F	54	68	46	62	53
Friends, Opposite Sex . . .	M	15	18	14	22	26
	F	30	32	33	57	25
Local Adults	M	19	20	15	20	24
	F	27	32	23	23	16
Teachers in General	M	38	37	24	20	18
	F	34	34	12	16	16
Other Academic Persons: (Counselors, coaches, principals)	M	9	9	6	13	15
	F	12	6	3	7	7
Unclassified: (e.g., God, famous people, dogs, me, etc.) . . .	M	28	22	18	25	16
	F	12	17	13	15	12

Figure 9.3
Academic Influence of "Significant Others"

Percentage of the Same Students at Each Grade Level Who Name at Least One Person in Each of the Following Categories of Significant Others as Being *Concerned About How Well They Do in School* (Males = 255 and Females = 306)

Categories of Others		Grade 8	Grade 9	Grade 10	Grade 11	Grade 12
Academic "Significant Others"	Sex	%	%	%	%	%
Parent (s)	M	96	97	96	95	96
	F	99	99	98	98	97
Age Level Relatives	M	19	30	20	26	29
	F	24	38	29	42	45
Adult Relatives	M	30	37	31	29	27
	F	45	55	41	52	31
Friends, Same Sex	M	5	8	6	10	11
	F	11	21	17	30	39
Friends, Opposite Sex . . .	M	4	7	5	13	21
	F	4	9	16	31	16
Local Adults	M	4	5	5	7	10
	F	6	11	7	14	19
Teachers in General	M	60	53	44	34	26
	F	63	50	35	35	29
Other Academic Persons: (Counselors, coaches, principals)	M	29	27	33	33	18
	F	37	33	33	33	32
Unclassified: (e.g., God, famous people, dogs, me, etc.) . . .	M	35	23	24	30	25
	F	37	30	32	22	25

Source:
From *Concept of Ability and School Achievement III* (Report of Cooperative Project, 2831) (p. 107) by W. B. Brookover, E. Erickson, L. Joiner, 1967, East Lansing: Michigan State Univ. Press.

These "significant others" may at times send out conflicting signals that will result in confusing the student and limiting achievement. For example, parents may state that they want their child to obtain above-average grades in school. At the same time, however, they stress the importance of his having a music proficiency. The amount of time required to succeed in both areas may appear unreasonable to the student. He may thus make a choice that is inconsistent with the actual desires of his parents. On the other hand, a student may sincerely believe that a parent desires a specific form of achievement but will ultimately be unaware of the success if he attains it. These apparent conflicting goals, therefore, will not initiate motivation.

Mendolsohn, Brookover, and Erickson identify parental involvement in school as correlated with levels of student achievement. For example, 65 percent of the parents who were highly involved in school related activities had children who were high achievers, but only 30 percent of the parents who were minimally involved in student academic affairs had children who were high achievers. On the other hand, 50 percent of the students who were low achievers had parents who were minimally involved in school affairs, and only 35 percent of the low achievers had parents who were highly involved in the school activities (Mendolsohn, 1972).

Research also shows that the expectations of the school personnel greatly influence student achievement. However, it must also be emphasized that our influence is effective only if the student believes that we are trustworthy and reliable. Students evidence powerful insight into the credibility of significant others. Consequently, if they do not trust our judgment, no deliberate attempt to influence their achievement will succeed.

At the beginning of this chapter, we emphasized the importance of each student in God's overall plan. We are responsible to God for helping our young people recognize this truth. We must accept and appreciate this responsibility and assist them in finding God's will for their lives and in preparing for the work He has for them. The world is full of people who are out of God's will and dissatisfied with how He made them. The Lord receives little glory from such lives. As Christian educators, and especially Christian counselors, we can not only help them accept themselves but also make the best use of the talents and opportunities the Lord has given them.

You will find that few students are incapable of improving their academic achievement. Since you as counselor have ready access to student records, you are in an excellent position to maintain an ongoing evaluation of student progress. We suggest that you try at least annually to establish a specific plan that will enable you to evaluate the apparent ability and achievement of each student.

The curriculum of a school is designed to meet the needs of those students expected to attend. The breadth of this program will vary with the number of students and the range of their abilities. All students accepted by a school should be able to find course work at a level of difficulty they can master while satisfying graduation requirements.

Because C-level students and below have a greater need for attention, you should spend more time with this group. By maintaining a master list of student enrollment that has available standardized test scores posted and by reviewing the report cards of each student at every report period, you will be able to identify those students whose performance is marginal or those who are not performing up to their potential. These students should be evaluated and appointments should be made with each student, along with his parents and/or teachers as it seems appropriate.

The focal point of all contact should be on encouraging the student to exert the effort required for him to perform up to the full level of his potential. We should, however, guard against establishing artificial goals and rewards. Lasting success will be best attained by making achievement its own reward. Parents and teachers who condition students to work for incentives other than learning itself will soon run out of "carrots." Rewards have a place, but they should not be used as a primary means of motivating the student.

It is impossible to tell a counselor how to use grades and test scores to establish specific goals for individual students. This is a matter that you as counselor must develop a feeling for in your particular situation. As you develop a profile for the student body using various available test scores, patterns will begin to emerge that will provide a basis for predicting individual student performance.

As you begin to work in academic counseling, you need to guard against being too specific and dogmatic about goals for individual subjects and students. Give basic direction and encouragement; the results will come, and experience will enable you to be more precise. Eventually, with your guidance, students will be able to establish their own goals. The important thing is to begin. Few schools have effective academic counseling programs. Yours should be an exception.

10 Vocational Guidance

Vocational guidance is a direct outgrowth of wise academic counseling. Consequently, when directing students in making career choices, we must keep in mind the same basic principles established in Chapter 9. We must be primarily concerned with directing the student in finding God's will, with helping him discern his God given abilities, and with encouraging him to use these talents for Christ.

Every young person faces three important decisions as he moves toward adult life: the demands of God for his sins, the choice of a mate (or for some the choice to remain single), and the choice of a vocation. The latter decision may in some ways affect the first two. Young people need to think seriously about their vocation because, for many, the preparation must begin at the high school level. Although early errors in judgment can usually be remedied, these errors may cause unnecessary financial strain and delay. This is especially true if the student decides to enter an area that requires specialized training.

A more serious danger, however, is the possibility that the student may be out of God's will. God is far more interested in what we are than in what we do; though, of course, if we are what we should be, we will do what we ought to do. Only when a young person is willing to follow God wholeheartedly is he in the position to receive direction. Therefore, the development of godly character is critical to career planning.

One of the saddest stories I know was told by a man who sponsored a youth group that I attended as a teenager. In giving his testimony, he told us that he had lived for over fifty years knowing that he was out of God's will. God had called him to be a missionary when he was young, but he had deliberately refused the call. He had rationalized that he could serve the Lord more effectively at home as a good Christian businessman. But at eighty he had to confess that, though he had always been an active

Christian, he had never known the true joy and genuine contentment of following God's will. How tragic it would be if those whom we counsel would in years to come make the same confession.

Career guidance begins when a student enrolls in your school. What he sees in your life, in the lives of other school personnel, and in fellow students will play a major part in influencing him to accept or reject the Lord's guidance. Both the school program and the school personnel should reflect a knowledge of the presence of God and a consciousness of His direction. If a student fails to see this, he is being taught through poor example to make his own choices apart from the Holy Spirit's leading. Once this pattern of thinking is established, it is difficult to alter.

One of the most effective methods of providing career guidance is through a special senior course. Many schools have such a course as a graduation requirement. A good topic of introduction for the course may be a study on "How to Find God's Will for Your Life." Team teaching is effective in this situation. For example, the pastor or associate pastor may teach the unit on the will of God. The guidance counselor could then follow up with a survey to determine student vocational interests. He could then develop and teach a second unit on the specific vocations compiled from the survey. Of course, this unit would include a thorough discussion of the major types of Christian service. We should never be ashamed to emphasize the need for personnel in God's work. This study of vocations should also include a consideration of the aptitude and training necessary for the individual careers. The possibilities for future development in each of the careers should also be discussed. The potential conflicts a Christian may face in individual vocations should also be addressed.

We must be careful to minimize the significance of financial potential. Young people need to understand that God has given us talents primarily to serve Him, not to make money. While financial considerations will eventually be a factor in their judgment, young people should not make vocational selections based on potential earnings.

Once the student focuses on one or two vocations, he needs help concerning the preparation required to enter each field. It is at this point that many counselors fail. We are responsible for familiarizing ourselves with the academic requirements for the various careers. We are then able to help the student honestly evaluate himself in light of these academic requirements. A student that expresses an interest in becoming a veterinarian but has difficulty in passing high school biology and chemistry should be directed to carefully evaluate his choice. Though it is not the role of the counselor to close the door to any field, he must not fail to point out inconsistencies between a student's academic performance in high school and the academic preparation required for the vocation of his choice.

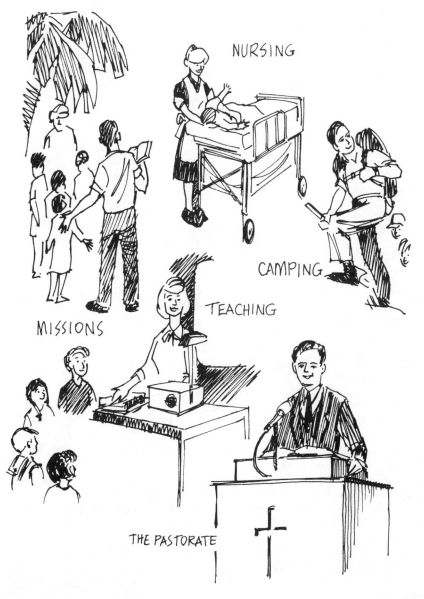

NURSING

CAMPING

TEACHING

MISSIONS

THE PASTORATE

Once a student has identified a general area of interest, we should not hesitate to call his attention to the ways that interest could be used in Christian work. For example, a student interested in forestry could work at a large Christian camp supervising the care of their grounds and assisting in nature instruction. A student interested in management or accounting could consider working as a business manager for a church, Christian school, or mission board. A nursing major could consider working at a Christian school, in a camping program, or on the mission field. A young man interested in automobile mechanics could consider teaching in a Christian technical school. Almost every type of vocation has some application to Christian work, and it is our responsibility to challenge our young people to consider *God's work first*.

Students also need to be reminded that the choice of a vocation is a lifelong commitment. Too many look only at the first few years. The job may look glamorous initially, but will it still look glamorous ten or fifteen years later? For example, they may find the benefits or location of the job appealing. Or they may be enamored with the attention or activity associated with the field. As counselors we must help them direct their focus to the right things. When we successfully motivate them to genuinely seek God's will, we will also be successful in directing their attention to the proper career considerations.

A special word of caution should be mentioned here about vocational counseling. Your role is to help students consider the options available to them. You should not force "your professional opinion" on them or allow them to put you in the position of making decisions for them. No one, not even their parents, should do that. The final decision is a matter between them and the Lord. Your job is to encourage them to be receptive to the Holy Spirit's guidance.

Our responsibilities as career counselors should not be taken lightly. We will frequently be asked to make suggestions to both students and parents about vocational choices. The information the school develops over the years will be invaluable in providing such counsel. Besides the results gleaned in student appraisal, some excellent materials on vocations have been developed by several publishers. We should be familiar with as much information as possible so that we might share this knowledge with others and provide appropriate direction for those entrusted to our care.

11 Educational Guidance

Once a student has settled on which vocation God desires for him, he is then ready to consider how and where to obtain further education. Though not all vocations require training beyond high school, careful consideration needs to be given to those that do. This choice of where to obtain further training may greatly influence the student's future marriage plans, choice of friends, associates, life style, and possibly even his geographical location. As a counselor you can play a key role in helping the student make the right choice.

The Bible clearly implies that we should take advantage of training that will prepare us for effective service (II Tim. 2:15). Though the primary emphasis in this passage is the study of God's Word, we must remember that all truth is God's truth; we must prepare ourselves to use this truth in whatever vocation we are led into.

Students needing additional training must choose from trade schools, junior colleges, four-year colleges and universities, and commercial educational institutions. A few high school graduates will choose employment with firms that require only a high school diploma. Most graduates from the typical Christian school will opt to continue their education beyond high school. Some will enroll in academic programs that offer associate degrees, but the majority will elect to pursue the bachelor's degrees.

Enrolling in an institution of higher learning gives the student new responsibilities, especially if he leaves his hometown. No matter how restrictive the school environment, the student will have to make decisions without the close support of parents and familiar surroundings. It is essential, therefore, that the school duplicate as nearly as possible the environment of the student's Christian home and that it offer a program consistent with the family's educational objectives for the student.

The above considerations should necessitate the student's refusing to place himself under the tutelage of unsaved instructors (Prov. 19:27). Education is inherently religious; thus, a teacher's religious views inevitably influence what he teaches. Though some areas of study are less subject to philosophic manipulation than others, none is completely immune (I Cor.2: 6-16, II Cor. 10:5). Consequently, a Christian young person should, whenever possible, seek training by Christian instructors in a Christian school.

Unfortunately, some Christians believe that it is better for a young person to receive an education in a secular institution. The supporters of this view state that students who are enrolled in Christian schools are being sheltered from the "real world." A just consideration of this rationale demands definitions for the terms *sheltered* and *real world.*

If we define sheltering as a means of protecting our young people from ideas and people that would cause them to stumble, then yes, Christian education seeks to shelter students. We want to protect them until they are adequately prepared to successfully deal with these pressures. No high school football coach would be foolish enough to permit his varsity team to scrimmage with a major college team. Likewise, we would be foolish to unnecessarily expose young Christians to Satan's onslaughts. Even those of us who are mature in the faith realize how effective Satanic attack can be. At no time in our lives can we throw caution aside (I Cor. 10:12). We, therefore, realize the value of Christian education as a means of conditioning students. We endeavor to methodically fortify them against the evil they must encounter. Actually, when we honestly evaluate this rationale, we can see that the world does a far more effective job of "sheltering" young people. They are extremely successful in shielding their students from the knowledge of God, His love for them, and their accountability to Him.

We must also evaluate the meaning of the phrase "real world." If by the *real world* we mean a place where God is viewed as a myth and man as a God, then yes, the Christian school shuts out the real world. If, however, we believe in God, in His present control, and in His ultimate return, then we realize that a Christian school is actually protecting the student from the world's distorted view of reality. We understand that a godly education is the only education that presents a true perspective.

What should we conclude about a Christian student's enrolling in a secular institution? If he truly wants to do the will of God, and if he is convinced of God's direct leadership into a vocation that requires training not offered in a Christian school, then, and only then, should he consider enrolling in a secular institution. He must be certain that when he places himself under the instruction of unsaved teachers that he is exactly where God wants him. Only then can he be confident that God will protect him from error. A student faced with the prospect of attending a secular school might consider enrolling in a Christian college for the first year or two of his training.

However, even selecting a college from among Christian schools can be difficult. A well-known national Christian school association recently recorded as many as 300 Christian colleges in the United States. This figure would, of course, include schools that exemplify a liberal definition of the word *Christian*. Students must, therefore, be cautioned to use the same spiritual discernment in choosing a Christian college that they would use in selecting a church. You, as the counselor, can greatly aid the student and his parents by listing the colleges offering the particular major he wants and by helping them see which of these are genuinely Christian. It is impossible for parents to be as knowledgeable about schools across the country as you should be. By having materials available and by helping them review the schools' programs, you will be providing a valuable service. Most Christian parents will appreciate your judgment and candid evaluation of the spiritual and academic quality of the schools under consideration.

Students who have not yet settled on God's will regarding their vocation should be advised to consider the colleges with the broadest range of opportunities. Also, those desiring to continue their education through or beyond the bachelor's degree will have a broader range of choices in Christian schools, but the field is still limited spiritually and must be approached cautiously.

Unfortunately, those young people who want vocational studies have very limited choices. Few Christian schools offer vocational training at either the secondary or post-secondary level. Most of the schools offering this training would not be considered genuinely Christian. Others offer little academically.

There are several factors that students and their parents must consider when choosing a college to attend. The following list of points may be helpful in narrowing the choices:

1. *Look for a school that has a distinctly fundamentalist tradition.* A nominally Christian school, one that has gradually given up its distinctly biblical heritage, is more threatening to a young Christian than an openly secular institution. In such an environment Satan can subtly catch the student off guard, confuse his thinking, and dilute his convictions.

2. *Look for a school that requires students to manifest a distinctly Christian testimony, both on and off the campus.* God is

not looking for part-time Christians; He is looking for sold-out young people determined to live for Him full-time. Seek a school totally committed to this type of training.

3. *Look for a school whose faculty/staff demonstrate the quality of Christian character you desire for your child.* We are not likely to climb higher than those we choose to follow. When you choose a college, you are in a sense limiting your child's development to the level of the people who make up the school.

4. *Look for a school that has a faculty qualified to offer the programs in its catalog.* People make the difference in an institution. While no faculty member who lacks dedication to Christ and His work is qualified to teach in a Christian school, no amount of dedication can be a substitute for a thorough knowledge of the subject matter. Both dedication and preparation are essential.

5. *Look for a school that offers a broad selection of courses, majors, and minors.* Few high school graduates know for certain what academic programs to pursue at the time of their graduation. Those enrolling in colleges with a wide range of academic opportunities to choose from are in the best position to be led of God into the specific study He desires for them.

12 Counseling Parents

Contact with parents is generally initiated for the following three reasons: to help the parents with their children, to help other family members needing counsel, and to establish an evangelistic outreach for the school.

Helping Parents with Their Children

Conflicting goals between parents and school leadership are a major obstacle to long-term success with young people. Counseling with parents can be one avenue of eliminating this obstacle and developing a harmonious relationship between the home and the school. Once established, this relationship will encourage an atmosphere of trust between parents and school staff and provide a greater opportunity for positively influencing the student. The school staff generally, and you as the counselor specifically, need to make a special effort to inform parents of your genuine interest and desire to help them meet the educational objectives and goals for their children.

By establishing open lines of communication with the parents, you can provide a basis for a better understanding of school rules and policies. You can also help parents discern any spiritual problems their children may be having and provide direction for further spiritual development. Also, as students enter high school, both they and their parents will benefit from specific information about high school graduation requirements, the various tracks available in the curriculum, and financial planning for higher education.

It is important to remember, however, that children are primarily the parents' responsibility (Deut. 6:6-9, Ps. 127:3, Eph. 6:1-4). Our role as Christian educators is simply to help parents fulfill this God-given responsibility. This caution applies not only to school personnel but also to youth pastors, Sunday school teachers, and others. Though we may be convinced that our approach in dealing with the student is correct and that the parents' approach is either incorrect or seriously limited, we must always be tactful. We can kindly point out errors and inconsistencies, but we have no right to impose our view on parents. We cannot usurp the authority God has given them over their children and expect Him to bless our efforts. This warning reemphasizes the importance of selecting and retaining students whose parents share the school's philosophy of Christian education.

Helping Other Family Members in Need

As a good counselor you will not only establish yourself as a friend to the student in need, but also as a friend to any of the student's family members who may need counsel. Parents who have observed your genuine love for their children will recognize that this same concern may be shown to them when they are in need.

Church schools are particularly well-situated for this additional counseling outreach, for the resources of the entire church staff are readily available to help resolve any problem of the parents. The nature of the problem, the sex of the parent, respective ages, your personal experience, and the parent's own desire are all considerations in whether you should work directly with the parent or refer him to another member of the church staff. You must remember, however, that the parents—one or both—may have approached you because of their confidence in you personally; consequently, they may resent or resist being referred to another person. In this case you should provide whatever assistance you can. If you are unprepared to handle the particular problem, you must at some point try to direct the parent to another staff member.

This referral should not be made, however, until the parents recognize that it will be beneficial. Following the referral, you should still inquire periodically about the parent's welfare and assure him or her of your continued interest. If you are a counselor in an independent school, you should not hesitate to involve the staff of good Bible-believing churches which support your school.

When dealing with these parental problems, you should take every opportunity to review the overall spiritual condition of each parent and the needs of the total family unit. Problems within the family are rarely limited to a single family member. You should pay particular attention to whether those seeking your assistance are born-again. Though we would not refuse aid to an unsaved person, we must realize that any help we give such a person will be superficial and temporary if his basic need of salvation is not met. You must first seek to lead such a person to Christ and help him realize that seeking forgiveness for sin and establishing a right personal relationship with God is an integral part of solving any problem. Your goal should be to work toward the establishment of a thoroughly Christian family. Never be content to deal only with the initial problem brought to your attention.

Children other than those enrolled in your school may also need counsel. When this comes to your attention, see it as an opportunity, not as an added burden. You will often find that the problems of other children in the family can contribute to any problems the enrolled student may be having.

Establishing an Evangelistic Outreach

Christian education is primarily for Christian children from Christian homes. Despite restrictive admissions policies there are bound to be some unsaved young people in your school. There will likewise be some unsaved family members of enrolled students. We cannot ignore or take lightly this potential evangelistic outreach. The student-parent-school relationship gives you an entrance into homes that would otherwise be closed. You will find that once parents have developed an appreciation for your school's ministry to their children, they seldom refuse to discuss with school or church representatives their personal spiritual needs.

You are the logical staff member to develop and coordinate much of this outreach to parents. Since you are already responsible for the maintenance of records, you have direct access to information that can identify families needing spiritual guidance. While it is not essential that you be solely responsible for this ministry, you will certainly want to be part of the team responsible for meeting this need. In a church school this program may be effectively organized under the leadership of the pastor and composed of not only the guidance counselor but also the youth pastor, visitation director, and associate or assistant pastor.

As counselor, you should prepare a list of prospects for church visitation based on these perceived needs. These needs could be determined through the initial interview, the application information, the teacher's perceptions and observations, and the direct contacts made with family members by the various school staff members. All school personnel should be alert for families needing a gospel witness, and a referral system should be established so that these families might be noted and contacted. Caution must be exercised, however, to be sure that evangelistic efforts do not appear as attempts to proselyte for church membership or school support. Members should not be solicited from other fundamental churches. If such soliciting takes place, the result will be a decline in support from other churches. Some families may at times move from other churches because of interest in the school, but this should not be encouraged.

The way in which the evangelistic outreach is organized and implemented varies. The structure of your school, the personnel available, personnel training, and additional responsibilities are all considerations in establishing the program. The important thing is to recognize that the opportunity exists, take advantage of the situation, and use it as a means of extending the Christian school ministry.

13 Records and Reporting

Understanding the need for keeping permanent or cumulative records is essential, for these documents will be used in making decisions about students long after those who have kept the records are unavailable for comment.

Maintaining Cumulative Records

Scripture provides several guidelines for maintaining records and for making certain that our records are accurate, objective, complete, and timely. The following references on this subject may be helpful to you: Ezra 4:15, Esther 6:1-3, Jer. 36:2-6, Luke 1:1-4, I Cor. 4:1, and I John 5:10-13.

Unfortunately, though most schools acknowledge the necessity of keeping records, many lack the commitment to maintain such records in an orderly fashion. In a well-organized school the supervision of collecting, organizing, and maintaining school records is the responsibility of a professionally trained counselor or other administrator. However, a recent survey of Christian school administrators and pastors with church related schools showed that in 44.8 percent of the schools, records were maintained by the secretary. In 26 percent of the schools, they were maintained by the principal, and in the remainder of the schools, no specific person was charged with the responsibility. It is not surprising then to see why some cumulative records require a miracle worker to decipher the array of information collected. In such cases anyone opening the folder is likely to find the following:

1. grade sheets yet unposted from the third grade. (The student is now in sixth grade but, the former secretary quit after his third grade year and the present secretary has not yet gotten around to up-dating the records.)

2. copies of notes from the student's mother requesting that the child be excused for an absence dating back to his first-grade year. (The secretary was not informed about when these notes could be disposed of; therefore, she kept them all filed in the cumulative record folder.)

3. whole test booklets from all the standardized achievement tests the student has taken since kindergarten. (No one thought of tearing off the booklet covers and disposing of the rest to save space or, still better, of designing a simple standardized-score-summary sheet on which all scores could be recorded.)

4. copies of all the notes the teachers have written to one another about the student along with notes to the student's parents about his failure to complete homework or copy his spelling words, about his fighting in the restroom and talking in class. (Useful information perhaps, but some of the notes are unsigned and/or undated prohibiting any chronological history being established—nor is there any indication that these problems were ever discussed with the student or any that specific effort was made to remedy the problem.)

5. further "pertinent" information loosely thrown into the already over-stuffed folder. (By now you should be getting an accurate picture of such record-keeping attempts.)

It's all there—every bit of information anyone would ever want to know along with much other insignificant information. The point is, that to be useful, student records need to contain a certain amount of specific information about the student, and this information needs to be arranged in a way that is easily accessible and beneficial to those who desire to use it.

Records may be maintained in a simple manila folder each bearing the name of a student. Another method is for records to be collected in a specially designed folder which includes a permanent record form. With this system the folder is used as the permanent record card and as the container for other data to be retained.

Contents of the Cumulative Record

The school is responsible for recording the enrollment, attendance, and academic progress of its students. Most schools find it useful to keep data beyond this minimum to enable them to provide further services to the student and his family. A typical Christian school cumulative record contains the following information:

1. Identifying data: student's name, names and address of parents, date and place of birth, citizenship if foreign born, spiritual condition, church affiliation and activities.
2. Health data: most states now require and provide a simple form for verification of immunizations and childhood illnesses (see Figures 13.1 and 13.2); results of routine vision, hearing, and dental examinations may also be retained.
3. Educational data: date of original enrollment; grade levels attended, courses taken, and grades received; promotions and failures; academic recognitions and awards received; the results of standardized tests of achievement and mental ability; also other standardized test data.
4. Observation data: copies of anecdotal and observation reports.
5. Discipline data: reports of any unusual disciplinary action; suspension, expulsion, probation, or limitation of activities; and refusal to grant re-admission.
6. Extra-curricular data: a record of involvement in school organizations, offices held, honors received, and participation in interscholastic sports.
7. Recommendation data: copies of any recommendations sent to prospective employers, the military services, colleges, etc. Schools with separate correspondence files may choose to place copies of recommendations in those files.

Figure 13.1

Sample Immunization Record

NAME: _____ BIRTH DATE: _____

IMMUNIZATION RECORD

Please Read Carefully:

The following vaccinations, immunizations, and/or screening tests are *required* by South Carolina law for all students attending schools within the state:

1. Diphtheria, Tetanus and Pertussis (DTP) Vaccine
   Three (3) doses of DTP (or adult Tetanus-Diphtheria, Td) vaccine.
   At least on DTP (or Td) dose is required after the fourth birthday.
   A booster of DT or Td is recommended every ten years.

2. Trivalent Oral Polio Vaccine (TOPV)
Three (3) doses of *oral* polio vaccine. At least one dose of oral polio vaccine is required after the fourth birthday.

3. Rubeola Vaccine
One (1) dose of rubeola vaccine administered after the first birthday. (Vaccine given *before* 1968 must be repeated.)

4. Rubella Vaccine
One (1) dose of rubella vaccine administered after the first birthday. Vaccination against rubella will not be required for females after the onset of puberty.

Please note these requirements:

1. There must be written proof of all vaccines.
2. The date must include day, month, and year.
3. There must be a date for *each* vaccine.
4. A physician's signature must be affixed to this record.

VACCINE	DATE	DATE	DATE	DATE	DATE
DPT					
DT					
POLIO, oral					
RUBEOLA (measles)					
RUBELLA (German measles)					
MUMPS (Recommended)					

I certify that the above named child received the listed vaccine doses or had a history of illness on the date(s) specified.

PARENT'S SIGNATURE   PHYSICIAN'S SIGNATURE

PARENT'S ADDRESS   DATE

Figure 13.2

Sample Immunization Exemption

South Carolina Department of Health and Environmental Control
South Carolina Certificate of Special Exemption
(From Immunization)

SECTION I - PUPIL INFORMATION

Pupil's Last Name	First Name	Initial	Name of School

Parent's Name	Address		Telephone

SECTION II - IMPORTANT INFORMATION FOR SCHOOL OFFICIALS

Pursuant to Section 44-29-40 of the South Carolina Code of Laws, 1976, Department of Health and Environmental Control Regulation 61-8, "A <u>South Carolina Certificate of Special Exemption</u>, signed by the school principal or his authorized representative, may be issued to transfer students while awaiting arrival of medical records from their former area of residence or to other students who have been unable to secure immunizations or documentation of immunizations already received. A <u>South Carolina Certificate of Special Exemption</u> may be issued only once and shall be valid for only thirty (30) calendar days from date of enrollment. At the expiration of this special exemption, the student must present a valid <u>South Carolina Certificate of Immunization</u>, or a valid <u>South Carolina Certificate of Medical Exemption</u>, or a valid <u>South Carolina Certificate of Religious Exemption</u>."

SECTION III - SCHOOL OFFICIAL'S CERTIFICATION OF SPECIAL EXEMPTION

Check ☑ the appropriate box below that best describes why this pupil is being issued a <u>South Carolina Certificate of Special Exemption</u>.If this pupil is being enrolled within the first thirty (30) days of the school year, a copy of this certificate must be attached to the 30-day report -- SCHOOL SUMMARY of STUDENT IMMUNIZATION STATUS, DHEC 1124. A copy of this certificate must be sent to the local health department upon enrollment when enrollment occurs after the first thirty (30) days of the school year.

☐ (FOR TRANSFER STUDENT) A thirty (30) day exemption from receiving any vaccines for a new student transferring into the school district from another district or area while awaiting arrival of medical records from former area of residence.

☐ (FOR NON-TRANSFER STUDENT) A thirty (30) day exemption due to delay in securing medical attention for immunizations or in securing documentation of immunizations already received.

_____   _____   _____
(Signature of School Official)   (Telephone)   (Date Certificate Issued)

1 ORIGINAL (School's Copy)   2 COPY (School to Send to Health Department)

DHEC 1123 (5-81)

Sources of Cumulative Record Information

Information for the cumulative record will come from three primary sources: enrollment and re-enrollment applications, grade sheets and/or report cards, and anecdotal and observation reports. Additional information will be supplied by organizations within the school and will be generated by special reports.

Enrollment and re-enrollment reports

A carefully designed application for enrollment and re-enrollment will contain most of the required information about the student and his family. This information can be copied from the application and put onto a specially prepared summary sheet; however, this process is time consuming and is not really necessary. It is simpler to file the application forms in the folder with the most recent form on top. Use a fastener to hold them neatly in place. This information can be updated annually as new applications are submitted.

For a minimum of three years, prior to the current year, the Internal Revenue Service requires non-profit schools to keep copies of all enrollment records and of all declined enrollment applications. In the case of declined application, the reason the applicant was rejected must be clearly stated. Figure 13.3 is a sample form illustrating the data required by the Internal Revenue Service and showing also some additional information that may be useful in projecting future enrollment patterns. Consult Appendix G for an example of how this information may be used in planning.

Figure 13.3

Weekly Enrollment Tally by Race

Enrollment statistics are broken down by the five racial categories: white (1), black (2), Hispanic (3), Asian or Pacific Islander (4), and American Indian or Alaskan Native (5).

Week	Category 1		Category 2		Category 3		Category 4		Category 5		Total
	(+)	(-)	(+)	(-)	(+)	(-)	(+)	(-)	(+)	(-)	
1	537		42		38		18		3		638
2											
3											
36											
Totals											

All schools operating on a non-profit tax-exempt basis are required to keep records on the enrollment, including its racial composition. Records do not require identification by name. This simple tally by week will enable a school to keep track of its enrollment throughout the year. The entries for week one represent the totals at the end of that week. For each remaining week of the year, enter the *net* gain or loss of students in each category by indicating (+) or (-) figure in the correct column. At the end of the year, simply bring down the *net* total category. This data will enable you to calculate the total enrollment, and the enrollment in all racial categories for any week in the school year.

At present the Internal Revenue Service is interested in determining whether your school's admission decisions are racially motivated. In the future, sexual preference, the sex of the individual, and other legislated Civil Rights areas may be of interest to them. At this point, schools are not required to identify students by race, but it is necessary that you be able to tell an auditor the racial breakdown of those applicants who were denied enrollment.

A file for declined applications should be established according to year. Applications for the entire year can then be discarded easily at the appropriate time. The applications should be filed alphabetically within the years so that your personnel can readily locate needed individual applications.

Grade Sheets and/or Report Cards

Two different approaches are commonly used to develop educational data. Once grades are posted on report cards, most schools require some type of grade sheet (see Figure 13.4) which is completed by the teacher and sent to the school office. Clerical office personnel are usually responsible for posting the individual grades on student records (see Appendix H for example of student record). This is obviously a time-consuming process, and therefore an expensive, tedious process. Its very nature leads to frequent errors. Unfortunately, since the elementary or secondary student and his parents rarely see the permanent record, the errors may go undetected.

Figure 13.4

Sample Grade Sheet

Student's Name

	Reading	Spelling	Geography	Bible	History	Science
1.						
2.						
3.						
4.						
5.						
6.						
7.						

There are advantages in using a report card designed on carbonless paper with the final copy on light-weight card stock (See Appendix I). Though initially more expensive, using this card reduces the chance of errors and the time required to record grades on permanent records. As the teacher records the student grades on the report card each grading period, they are simultaneously recorded on the permanent record card. The top sheet is torn off each grading period and sent home with the student. At the end of the year, the teacher simply sends the card to the office to be placed in the student's cumulative record file. If designed on 8-1/2-inch x 11-inch stock, the form is convenient for filing and lends itself to easy duplication on a plain paper copier. If the form is appropriately designed, the scoring labels from yearly standardized tests can also be placed on the office copy. When a student record is requested by another school, use one sheet of paper per grade level and copy the following: the record card, a complete record of attendance, courses taken, grades received, standardized test scores, and promotion or retention notations. The initial higher cost for forms is quickly recovered in reduced personnel cost for the processing of information.

Establishing A Filing System

Filing cumulative records is an important consideration. Several approaches may be taken, all of which work reasonably well.

Traditionally records have been maintained in folders that were then stored in steel file cabinets. Most records are still stored in this way, although there are now more attractive, efficient, and modern systems available. If you are preparing to establish new records, it would be to your advantage to visit an office equipment supply company and ask for a demonstration of the filing equipment currently available.

Records should be divided into at least two categories: present or currently enrolled students and former students. Within these categories the records should be filed alphabetically. As your school grows and the number of records increases, you will see the wisdom of this approach. Many schools further divide the records of present students by grade level. This division is helpful when looking at some aspect of progress involving students in a particular grade or class. They would, of course, be alphabetically arranged within each grade level.

Schools are increasingly using microcomputers to reduce the burden and increase the efficiency, accuracy, and speed of processing student data. Equipment now available is both suitable and reasonably priced. If this method is used, however, schools must plan to insure the security and confidentiality of the records. You should also provide duplicate records in the event that those in the computer are destroyed. Frequently, those using the computer to store and generate reports on student data also plan to have computer print-outs of the reports available which are filed as traditional school records. These are updated periodically.

Some schools, particularly smaller ones, file all correspondence in the student's cumulative record folder. While this facilitates filing, the overall merits are open to question. For example, if a family has more than one child in the school, in which child's folder is the correspondence to be placed? If it is decided to place the correspondence in the oldest child's folder, will the secretary remember to move the correspondence when that child leaves the school? What happens if the secretary is not familiar enough with the family or simply forgets that there is more than one child in the family? It is preferable to set up a separate correspondence file for each family. If correspondence is kept in the cumulative folder, be certain none of it is sent to another school in the event a record is requested. This correspondence should be removed from the folder and destroyed or transferred to another place when the student leaves the school.

You should also make certain that you have a backup system for your records. Though unlikely, it is possible that the original documents could be destroyed in some disaster. Using microfilm is the easiest and least expensive method for providing such a system. You could microfilm the records each summer and keep copies of this film in a separate place. If, however, you are unable to use microfilm, you could photocopy the records and store these copies in a safe location separate from the original documents.

Preparation of Transcripts

The school is responsible for information on students for the entire period of their enrollment at the institution. It is customary for the last elementary or secondary school a student attended to make the complete academic records available upon request to whoever is entitled to them. (See Figure 13.9 for a list of elements of an elementary and/or secondary school transcript.) Consequently, cumulative records need to indicate clearly what school the student attended at a given time. Original documents should not be sent when the records are requested by another school. Photocopies and forms specially designed for the purpose should be used. Failure to follow this procedure places the institution in jeopardy if another institution should in the future request the student record. The only exception to this rule is made in the case of some foreign students. Some countries commonly send the original record with the student. If you are given the original records of a foreign student, these original records should, upon his request, be sent on to another school. Prior to sending them, however, you should make copies of the original documents for future reference.

Figure 13.5

Elements of an Elementary/Secondary Transcript

The following information should be considered the minimum content reported on any secondary level student. Normally when a student finishes high school and requests a transcript, he wants a report on work taken in grades nine and above only. That is all that should be sent unless the record for earlier years is specifically requested. Points 1-7, 9-15, 25, 26, 30, 31, 34-39 would apply to elementary transcripts.

Student Identification

1. Student's full legal name
2. Sex
3. Birthdate
4. Birthplace (country is sufficient for foreign students)
5. Student's Social Security number (will be required by most colleges)

School Identification

6. Complete name and mailing address
7. Telephone number (including area code)
8. School's CEEB and ACT code numbers
9. Name and title of person who should be contacted concerning verification of school records
10. Name of the principal

General Information About the School (see Appendix J)

11. Describe school organization, ownership, and purpose
12. Brief statement of philosophy
13. Grades or school years offered
14. Brief history
15. Total enrollment, enrollment pattern
16. Size of graduating class
17. Number and description of faculty
18. School year (beginning and ending dates of current year, number of school days, length of school day)
19. Grading system
20. Method of computation GPA (what, if any, subjects are excluded from computation) and class rank
21. Graduation requirements
22. Percentage of graduating class that goes on to college
23. Any special honors students have earned that would be noteworthy
24. Results of recent ACT and/or SAT examinations (median score)

Student's Academic History

25. List of all courses taken and grade or other evaluation
26. Courses should be grouped by year
27. Courses should indicate unit value
28. Total credits accumulated towards graduation as of transcript date
29. Any courses taken in grades nine and above that are not high school level should be so indicated
30. Any courses taken by correspondence or by some means different from the manner instruction is normally given (independent study, for example) should be so indicated
31. Courses in progress at the time the transcript is issued should be listed
32. Grade point average and/or rank in class

33. Date of student's graduation (or anticipated graduation)
34. Date student entered school
35. Names and addresses of other schools the student attended (courses taken at these schools should be clearly identified)
36. Results of standardized achievement and/or mental ability tests (scores, dates administered, and name and form of test should be indicated)
37. Special features of a student's program (special education, vocation, general, college preparatory, etc.)
38. Signature and title of person certifying transcript

Student's Personal Characteristics

39. Significant in-school and out-of-school accomplishments
40. A statement concerning the student's potential particularly for colleges considering the student for admission
41. A general recommendation (optional)

The preceding information is based on the recommendations of the National Association of Secondary School Principals

---

Once students have completed high school, records requested for them are normally confined to grades nine through twelve. Schools usually design a special form to consolidate data covering these years. It may be presented concisely in one or two 8 1/2 x 11-inch pages (for example see Appendix K).

In addition to the information discussed earlier in this chapter, it is customary for schools to calculate and report the student's rank in class. This information is frequently requested by colleges as a basis for comparing the student with other members of his graduating class. It is helpful to know the size of the class and the student's relative position within the group. Rank in class should be calculated after graduation. Because some colleges require this information before acting on the student's application for admission, it is not uncommon for schools to calculate tentative class rank sometime during the student's senior year.

A school transcript is an important document. We cannot overestimate the importance of ensuring total accuracy in the transcripts.

Transcripts must be certified by someone in the school that has been delegated this authority. The official transcript should have the school seal impressed on it. To avoid alteration, official transcripts should be sent directly from the school to the individual or institution requiring them. Transcripts given to students should be stamped "Issued to Student" and should not bear the institutional seal. They should also be dated.

A school that is a ministry of a church may use the corporate seal of the church or may have a school seal prepared. Independent schools would, of course, have their school corporate seal. Seals are available through any office supply company. A place for the certification and the seal is normally designed into the transcript (see Appendix K).

Summary

Summary

14 Providing Essential Services Without a Guidance Counselor

The first thirteen chapters of this book have been written with the assumption that your school has the services of a part-time or a full-time guidance counselor with experience and/or training for the position. As we observed in the first chapter, however, this will not be true in many Christian schools.

We hope you have become convinced of the value of a trained counselor on the school staff and will plan to employ one as soon as possible. Some will want to make this move immediately but will be unable to rearrange their priorities or to persuade their superiors to make the necessary financial commitment at this time. If you find yourself in this position, what can you do?

There are several alternatives to consider. The first step is to conduct an audit to determine how well your school is performing in pupil personnel services. If possible, this audit should be done by an individual who is knowledgeable in pupil personnel services but is not part of your organization. A faculty member at a Christian college or an associate at another Christian school would be ideal. If, however, you cannot find an appropriate person, make an effort to do it yourself. Remember, if the audit is to be profitable, you must be honest and uncompromising. The following areas that were listed in the first chapter should be considered: orientation, counseling, educational and vocational planning, informational services, child study and testing, curriculum study, job placement, follow-up program, and the keeping of student records.

Though you are likely to find that some of these areas are well managed, others will reflect moderate or serious problems, and one or two of the areas will be completely lacking or non-existent.

Once you have completed your audit, take an honest look at the results. If the audit was done by an outsider, discuss it thoroughly. Resist the temptation to set it aside or to conclude that the situation is not as bad as it seems. Immediately begin developing a list of actions that will be taken to remedy the problems. Be realistic. Set up priorities. You probably cannot correct all the problems right away, perhaps not even by next year. The important point is to understand what must be done to have a quality program and prepare to move in that direction. Work on the most important areas and on those that can be accomplished with a minimum of effort and expense. This will give you a sense of progress and satisfaction and encourage you to continue. You will find that some things can be corrected by simply establishing a new policy or slightly revising an existing one. Others will require the training or retraining of personnel, or in some cases the employment of personnel and/or the purchasing of equipment and materials. Do not allow the list to overwhelm you; take the task in stride and patiently attack one problem after another.

Begin immediately to obtain resources in pupil personnel services. Obtain books, subscribe to professional journals, and find other aids that will help you and your staff in understanding the value and responsibilities of a pupil personnel program. A suggested list of reference materials is provided in Appendix L, in addition to those listed in the bibliography.

Consider taking courses at a college or university yourself or sending someone else on your staff. Perhaps an outsider could provide immediate aid by giving you or other members of your staff some in-service training. Formal training will enable you to quickly bridge the knowledge gap. Seek help in selecting the right courses, for some classes will obviously be of more immediate help than others. Remember, however, that these procedures are temporary measures. We are not interested in making the pastor or principal of the school a guidance counselor. Both of these people have more than enough to do in their present positions. Our objective is to put the school in the best possible position to provide the needed services and to upgrade as quickly as possible those already in the program.

It might also be productive to take another look at each of the pupil personnel services listed and consider the personnel currently assigned to these duties. It may be that most of the people were assigned responsibilities because they were available, not because of their ability, training, or interest. Figure 14.1 makes suggestions on how these responsibilities might be delegated in a typical church-related school.

Figure 14.1

Pupil Personnel Service Assignments
for Schools Without Counselors

SERVICE	RESPONSIBILITY
COUNSELING ORIENTATION ➡	PASTOR ASSOCIATE/ASSISTANT PASTOR
ORIENTATION JOB PLACEMENT INFORMATIONAL SERVICES CURRICULUM STUDY ➡	PRINCIPAL
EDUCATIONAL AND VOCATIONAL PLANNING CHILD STUDY AND TESTING FOLLOW-UP PROGRAM ➡	VICE-PRINCIPAL/ ASSISTANT PRINCIPAL/ SUPERVISOR
STUDENT RECORDS ➡	SECRETARY

How the responsibilities are divided is not as important as the overall rationale supporting your decisions. When delegating these duties, consider the stated preferences of your personnel, their professional training and experience, and their spiritual maturity and spiritual gifts. Remember, the lives of many students will be affected by these important choices.

Appendix

Appendix A Sample School Brochure

Thunder Mountain Christian School

19___/19___

Educational Kindergarten
(5 yr.)through Twelfth Grade

Thunder Mountain Christian School

1000 Waterway Blvd.
Anytown, Co. 76432
Telephone: (area code)000-0000

A ministry of Thunder Mountain Baptist Chruch

If you believe. . .

That your children need to think for themselves, rejecting all wisdom of the past including God's Word. . .

That your children should develop a spirit of independence, making their own plans for the future regardless of God's will. . .

That your children should develop their *creativity*, "doing their own thing" no matter whom they hurt. . .

Then you do not want a Christian education.

But if you want your children to develop. . .

God-given abilities
Strength of character
Appreciation of hard work
Initiative
Honesty
Right thinking
Love of God and country. . .

Then THUNDER MOUNTAIN CHRISTIAN SCHOOL is for you!

Financial Information

Tuition		11 Payments
Educational Kindergarten		
Each Student	$682	$62
Grades 1 through 9		
One child	$902	$82
Second child and each additional child in family	$682	$62
Grade 10-11		
Each Student	$902	$82

Tuition payments are due in advance by the first of each month beginning August 1st and ending with the last day of school. A statement will be mailed to you about the 25th of each month.

Application and Enrollment Fees

New Students—An application fee of $50 will be charged for each application considered. No action will be taken on an application until application fees have been paid. When you are advised that your children have been accepted, the supply fees must be paid within 15 days to insure a place in the grade. THE APPLICATION FEE IS NOT REFUNDABLE.

Old Students—An application fee of $30 will be charged for each student considered for re-enrollment. In addition, a $40 deposit will be required with the re-enrollment fees PER FAMILY. The $40 deposit will be applied to the fees due August 1st. THE RE-ENROLLMENT FEE IS NOT REFUNDABLE. If for any reason a student who applies for re-enrollment is not accepted in the school, both the re-enrollment and deposit fees will be refunded. The deposit will also be refunded if written notice of the parent's intent not to send their children is received by June 1.

Supply and Book Fees

An annual supply fee of $50 will be charged for each student enrolled in the school. Supply fees for new students will be due when advised of acceptance. Supply fees for students re-enrolling will be due August 1st. This fee will cover the cost of textbook rental, workbooks, and materials. Students will be expected to provide their own paper, pencils, and notebooks.

Bus Fees

One child in the family	$30/month for 10 months
Second child and each additional child in the same family	$15/month for 10 months

An additional fee of $5 per month will be charged any family living more than 10 miles from the school.

Laboratory Fees

A fee of $25 will be charged all students taking biology, advanced biology, chemistry, or physics. These fees will be payable Oct. 1st.

A form of the complete financial policy is available in the school office.

A Brief History

Thunder Mountain Christian School was founded as a ministry of the church in 1967. The primary purpose of the school was and is to assist parents in training their children according to biblical standards. Initially the school offered only kindergarten through grade eight, but grades nine through twelve were added in 1969. Enrollment for 1983/84 was 661 with a graduating class of 42.

Admission Policy

1. A written application for enrollment must be submitted with appropriate fees.

2. To be accepted above the first-grade level, students must earn a minimum score on a standard entrance exam. The academic program of the school is designed for average and better students. Students who are unable to do average work may be asked to withdraw. No provisions are available for mentally or emotionally handicapped children or for children with severe learning disabilities.

3. No student will be considered for enrollment who is two years above the chronological age for the grade level.

4. Students must reach the chronological age required for a given grade by September 1st in order to be placed in that grade.

5. Parents must agree to submit their children to the discipline and overall program of the school as outlined in detail in the Student-Parent Handbook.

Notice of Nondiscriminatory Policy for Students

Thunder Mountain Christian School admits students of any race, color, national, or ethnic origin to all rights, privileges, programs, and activities generally accorded or made available to the students at the school. It does not discriminate on the basis of race, color, national, or ethnic origin administration of its educational policies, admissions policies, scholarship and loan programs, or athletic or other school administered programs.

Curriculum

The school offers a standard academic program. All essential academic subjects are included and are taught at the appropriate grade levels. The Bible is taught as an academic subject and is also integrated into other subjects. Thunder Mountain Christian School strives for academic and spiritual excellence. Students are expected to do their best. Those who do not, may not be permitted to re-enroll.

Location

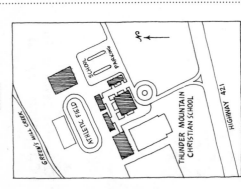

Discipline and Conduct

High standards of conduct are required of all those associated with Thunder Mountain Christian School. All students and faculty are required to dress in a manner consistent with a separated Christian testimony. Girls in grades seven and above must wear dresses or skirts no shorter than knee length. In grades five and six, they must not be more than two inches above the knee. Boys' hair is to be neatly trimmed and cut in a conventional way. Extremes in fashion are discouraged for boys and girls alike because they tend to draw attention to the individual rather than the Saviour we are called to serve. Any student consistently in conflict with any policy of the school will be asked to withdraw.

Biblical Position

The Word of God is the final source for our instruction in spiritual matters. Doctrinal teaching is consistent with the historic Baptist position. Thunder Mountain Christian School has a two-fold Bible emphasis: to show each student his need of Jesus Christ as his personal Saviour and to present the Bible as God's absolute standard for moral conduct. For the sake of uniformity and in keeping with our position of the inerrancy of the Scriptures, only the King James Version of the Bible is used.

Purpose

The primary purpose of Thunder Mountain Christian School is to give each student the maximum knowledge of secular subjects and the essentials of culture in the light of God's Word. "That in all things He might have the preeminence" (Col. 1:18). Even though knowledge is factually the same for the believer and unbeliever, no subject can be taught in its truth if its originator is ignored. Recognizing that spiritual truths are spiritually discerned, only teachers who have personally accepted Jesus Christ as their Saviour and Lord can possibly teach in a way pleasing to God. Consequently, only a Christian school, with born-again teachers can give a child the education God expects in keeping with His instruction in Proverbs 22:6: "Train up a child in the way he should go: and when he is old, he will not depart from it." Our entire school program is designed to help parents fulfill this command of God. Any parent with different educational and spiritual expectations for his children is likely to be dissatisfied with Thunder Mountain Christian School.

Academic Status

The administrative staff and the instructional staff of Thunder Mountain Christian School are well qualified to perform their work. All faculty members are required to be certified by the American Association of Christian Schools and/or the State Association of Christian Schools. Achievement tests administered annually show our student body to be performing above the national average. The school is accredited by the American Association of Christian Schools. Students who have done well here move easily into other private and public schools locally and across the nation.

Appendix B Sample Handbook Format

Student-Parent Handbook

I.   Introduction
    A. History of the School
    B. Purpose of the School
    C. School Colors, Mascot, Song
II.   Admissions
    A. Statement of Nondiscrimination
    B. Testing
III.   Academics
    A. Accreditation
    B. Curriculum
    C. Homework
    D. Grading/Promotion
    E. Scholarship
IV.   Conduct and Discipline
    A. Dress and Hair Code
    B. Conduct Rules
    C. Disciplinary Penalties
V.   Services
    A. Bus
        1. Schedule
        2. Rules
        3. Patrol Guards
    B. Food
VI.   Fees
VII.   General Policies and Information
    A. Hours
        1. School
        2. Office
    B. Attendance
    C. Parent Involvement
        1. Parent-Teacher Fellowships
        2. Parent-Teacher Involvement
        3. Visiting the School
    D. Use of Telephone
    E. Student Drivers
    F. Sickness, Injury, and Medication
    G. Cancellation Days
VIII.   Student/Parent Agreement Clause

Appendix C Sample Handbook Format

Faculty Handbook

I.   Introduction
   A. Philosophy of Education
   B. Introduction to the School
      1. History
      2. Purpose
      3. Organization
         (including church-school related relationship)
      4. Doctrinal Position
II. Employment Policies
   A. Basis for Employment
   B. Financial Arrangments
   C. Benefits
      1. Insurance
      2. Educational Grants
      3. Tuition Discounts
      4. Retirement Program
III. Personnel Regulations
   A. Standards
      1. Personal Appearance
      2. Promptness
   B. Schedule
      1. Hours
      2. Prayer Meeting
      3. Other Meetings
      4. Tutoring
   C. Paid Time Off
      1. Breaks
      2. Absences
         (including responsibilities when absent)
      3. Special Requests
IV. Academic Policy
   A. Accreditation and Certification
   B. Admissions
      1. Admissions Policy
      2. Testing
      3. Scholarships
   C. Curricula
      1. Elementary
      2. Junior High
      3. Senior High

D. Reporting
  1. Report Cards
  2. Promotion
  3. Graduation
V. Parent-Student Relationships
  A. Meeting
    1. Grade-Level Meetings
    2. Parent-Teacher Conferences
    3. Parent-Teacher Conferences
  B. Discipline
    1. Minor Disciplinary Action
    2. Suspension
    3. Expulsion
VI. Spiritual Responsibilities
VII. Teaching Policies and Suggestions
  A. Daily Schedule
    1. Class Schedule
    2. Preparation for the Day
    3. Lesson Plans
    4. Arrival/Late Arrival
    5. Beginning the Day
    6. Pledges
    7. Attendance Records
      a. Excused Absences
      b. Unexcused Absences
      c. Tardiness
  B. Building Policies
    1. Classroom Rules
    2. Moving in the Building
    3. Restrooms
    4. Food Service
    5. Safety Precautions
    6. Mailboxes
    7. Hall Bulletin Board
    8. General Maintenance
    9. Library
    10. Study Hall
  C. Supplies and Equipment
    1. Requesting Supplies
    2. Purchasing Supplies
    3. Using Supplies
      a. Audiovisuals
      b. Bulletin Boards

       c. Duplicating Service
       d. Books
       e. Typewriter
  D. Special Activities
    1. Scheduled
       a. First Day
       b. Getting to Know the Students
       c. Classroom Checklist (beginning of year)
       d. Field Trips
       e. Parties
       f. Checkout List (end of year)
       g. Awards
    2. Unscheduled
       a. Fire and Tornado Drills
       b. Illness and Accidents

Appendix D Sample Application

THUNDER MOUNTAIN CHRISTIAN SCHOOL
1000 Waterway Blvd
Anytown, CO 76432
APPLICATION FOR ADMISSION

GENERAL INFORMATION

Full Legal Name: _____
Last or Family Name

_____
First   Middle   (Name by which called)

Check semester for which you are making application:
☐ Fall   19 _____
☐ Spring   19 _____

Are you applying for a dormitory reservation? ☐ yes   ☐ no
(All students must live in the dormitories unless they are married or live nearby with close relatives.)

Social Security Number: _____

Sex: ☐ Male   ☐ Female

Race (check the *one* which best applies to you):
☐ White   ☐ Asian or Pacific Islander
☐ Black   ☐ American Indian or Alaskan Native
☐ Hispanic

Date of Birth: _____

Place of Birth: _____
City   State

Citizenship (country): _____

Telephone Number: (_____) _____
Area Code   Number

Parent's Telephone Number: (_____) _____
(If different from yours)   Area Code   Number

Present Mailing Address:

_____
Number   Street

_____
City   State   Zip

Permanent Home Address:

_____
Number   Street

_____
City   State   Zip

County (not country): _____

Father's Name: Mr.
Rev. _____
Dr.   *(Indicate deceased if not living)*

Permanent Address: _____

_____

Mother's Name: Mrs.
Dr. _____
(Indicate deceased if not living)

Permanent Address: _____

_____

DO NOT WRITE IN THIS SPACE

DATE _____ BY _____

ATTN. OF _____

ATTD. TO _____

CHECKED _____

Have you ever been a student in Thunder Mountain Christian School?
☐ yes   ☐ no

If so, when? _____

Check your present marital status:
☐ Single   ☐ Divorced*
☐ Married   ☐ Divorced and remarried*
☐ Widow or widower

*If this status is checked, letter of explanation must accompany the application.

Do you plan to be married before the time of enrollment?
☐ yes   ☐ no

If you are married (or will be before enrollment), give wife's or husband's name:

_____
Last   First   Middle

and race:
☐ White   ☐ Asian or Pacific Islander
☐ Black   ☐ American Indian or Alaskan Native
☐ Hispanic

Has he or she ever been enrolled in Thunder Mountain Christian School?
☐ yes   ☐ no

If you are a married woman, give full maiden name:

_____

Give names of members of your immediate family who have attended Thunder Mountain Christian School.

_____
Name   Relationship

_____
Name   Relationship

Are you a church member?   ☐ yes   ☐ no

Give *specific* denomination: _____

If Baptist, check one:
☐ Baptist Bible Fellowship   ☐ GARB
☐ Free Will Baptist   ☐ Other

Full name and address of church where membership is held:

_____
Name

_____
Street or P.O. Box

_____
City   State   Zip

Name of Pastor: _____

Appendix D

Do you attend church regularly? ☐ yes ☐ no

If so, is it the same church as above? ☐ yes ☐ no

If different, give *specific* denomination: _____

If Baptist, check one:
☐ Baptist Bible Fellowship ☐ GARB
☐ Free Will Baptist ☐ Other

Give full name and address of church you attend:

_____
Name

_____
Street or P.O. Box

_____
City State Zip

Name of Pastor: _____

Are you now or have you ever been under the supervision of a parole officer or under the custody of a juvenile or other court?
☐ yes ☐ no

Have you ever had a police record? ☐ yes ☐ no

If yes, give dates. _____
(If answer to either of the above questions is affirmative, give full information, including the name and address of the judge or probation officer, on the back of this application.)

Have you ever served in the United States Armed Forces?
☐ yes ☐ no

If so, give the dates: from _____ to _____

If you have been separated from such service, state the nature of such separation, and, if other than honorable, specify the type and the circumstances of your release.*

_____

If you have not yet been separated, state your expected date of release.

_____

*It is each applicant's responsibility to see that a copy of his discharge documents (DD-214) is sent to our office.

EDUCATIONAL BACKGROUND

Were you ever expelled, dropped, or suspended by any school?
☐ yes ☐ no
If answer is affirmative, state details, including name of school, time, and reason for such action on the back of this application.

Name and address of high school you are now attending or of last high school in which you were enrolled:

_____
Name of School

_____
Number Street

_____
City State Zip

List any other high schools you have attended and give the addresses: _____

_____

_____

_____

RESERVATION INFORMATION

Check the grade you expect to enter:
☐ Ninth ☐ Eleventh
☐ Tenth ☐ Twelfth

To whom should your statement for account be sent?
☐ self ☐ guardian
☐ mother ☐ other
☐ father

If other, give complete name and address of person to whom the statement should be sent:

_____
Name

_____
Street or P.O. Box

_____
City State Zip

HEALTH INFORMATION

A medical record must be in our files before a student is finally and definitely accepted. This information is secured by means of a questionnaire which will be provided to each applicant after his application has been submitted. A chest x-ray and several laboratory procedures will be administered upon the student's arrival on our campus.

Do you have any physical limitations which might require some adjustment to a normal student activity schedule?
☐ yes ☐ no

If so, please describe. _____

Are you presently taking regularly any medication prescribed by a physician? ☐ yes ☐ no

If so, give medication and frequency. _____

For what condition? _____

Have you been hospitalized within the past year?
☐ yes ☐ no

If so, give dates _____ and reason for hospitalization. _____

Have you ever been treated for any nervous, mental, or emotional disorder? ☐ yes ☐ no

If so, over how long a period? _____
and when? _____ Give the name and address of attending physician or psychiatrist:

Name _____

Address _____

_____

Have you ever used marijuana, narcotics, or dangerous drugs?
☐ yes ☐ no

If so, state on the back of this application the drugs used, dates used, the number of times used, and the last date you used them.

FINANCIAL RESPONSIBILITY

I hereby make application for admission to Thunder Mountain Christian School and enclose the $25 application fee with the understanding that the fee will be retained to cover the cost of processing my application. I understand that my application will be processed, and I will be notified when my records are ready to be submitted to the Admissions Committee. Within three weeks of the time I receive such notification, I will pay the $75 matriculation fee, which is refundable only if later information forces Thunder Mountain Christian School to refuse my application.

I understand that, if I request any change in my reservation after one week prior to the official opening of the term for which application is made (a change in housing or marital status), I will incur a fee of $50 to offset the cost of handling such changes by hand. I also understand that this charge will apply if I make application after this time or if I fail to cancel my reservation prior to this time. If I leave before the end of the semester for any reason whatever (either voluntary withdrawal or expulsion), I will owe the tuition and fees for the semester and the room and board through the current school month. In the event of said termination, I will not expect my transcript or other school records to be released until full payment is made. If I do not cancel my reservation for second semester by one week prior to the opening of the second semester, I will owe a fee of $50. This agreement carries over from year to year. If I should be accepted, I agree to give cheerful and ready obedience to and cooperation with the spirit and regulations of Thunder Mountain Chrisitian School.

I hereby declare on my word of honor that I have not omitted the name of any school in which I was ever registered, even for a brief period, and that I have answered all of the above questions truthfully and fully. Further, I give Thunder Mountain Christian School my approval to gather data from all schools which I have attended, together with other records and references that it believes to be necessary for the processing of my application.

_____   _____
Date   Signature of Applicant

The parent or legal guardian of the student making application must sign in the space provided below.

As parent or legal guardian of the above applicant, I agree to cooperate with Thunder Mountain Christian School in the enforcement of the rules and regulations of the insitiution and to meet the terms of the agreement about expenses, business details, etc., as outlined by Thunder Mountain Christian School.

_____
Signature of Parent or Legal Guardian

If signature is that of legal guardian, the following information is necessary:

Name of Guardian _____ Address _____

(continue on back if necessary)

PLEASE CHECK APPLICATION CAREFULLY.
ALL QUESTIONS MUST BE ANSWERED AND APPLICATION FEE MUST BE SUBMITTED BEFORE APPLICATION CAN BE CONSIDERED OR PROCESSED.

Appendix E Helpful References for Counseling Problems

The Christian school guidance counselor will be called upon to assist students, their parents, and other members of the church and school constituency with a wide range of spiritual problems. The following headings are a list of problems frequently encountered in counseling situations. Following each heading are several Scripture references you may find helpful when dealing with these specific problems. The list is not intended to be an exhaustive treatment of what the Bible has to say on these subjects, but it will provide a starting place for the counselor.

Alcohol, Drugs, and Tobacco

Proverbs 20:1; I Corinthians 3:16, 17; 6:12-20; Ephesians 5:18; Galatians 5:16-25; Revelation 21:8; 22:14, 15

"Sorcery comes from the Greek word *pharmekeia* and refers to one who prepares drugs for religious purposes" (Collins, 1980, p. 393).

Anger

Proverbs 14:17, 29; 15:1, 18; 19:11; 20:22; 22:24; 25:28; 29:11; Ephesians 4:26-32; James 1:19, 20

Anxiety

Psalm 55:22; Proverbs 17:22; Matthew 6:25-34; Philippians 4:6, 7; I Peter 5:7; I John 4:16-18

Companions

Proverbs 9:6; 13:20; 22:24; 29:24; Romans 16:17, 18; I Corinthians 5:9-13; II Corinthians 6:14-18

Conversation

Proverbs 10:18; 11:13; 26:20; Ephesians 4:25-32; James 3:5-10; 4:11

Death

Psalm 23; 116:15; Proverbs 14:32; John 14:1-6; I Corinthians 15:54-58; Philippians 1:21-23; Hebrews 2:14, 15

Depression

Genesis 4:6, 7; Psalm 32; 38; 43; 51; 68; 88; 102; Proverbs 18:14; Matthew 5:12; 11:28-30; John 15:9-12; Romans 15:13; II Corinthians 4:6-10; Philippians 4:11; Hebrews 13:5

Discipline

Proverbs 3:11, 12; 19:18; 22:15; 23:13, 14; 29:15; I Corinthians 11:29-34; Hebrews 12:5-11

Doubt

Proverbs 14:26; Isaiah 30:15; Ephesians 3:11, 12; James 1:6-8; I John 3:18-24; 5:14, 15

Envy

Titus 3:1-7; James 3:14-16; I Peter 2:1-3; Romans 13:13

Family Problems

Genesis 2:18, 24; Exodus 12; Ephesians 6:1-4; Colossians 3:20, 21; I Timothy 3:4, 5; I Peter 3:8-17

Fear

Proverbs 3:24-26; 14:26, 27; 29:25; Isaiah 14:3; Matthew 10:26-31; Romans 8:14-16; II Timothy 1:7; I Peter 3:13-15; I John 4:18

Finances

Psalm 49:10-12; Proverbs 23:4, 5; 27:24; Malachi 3:8-11; Matthew 6:25-34; 25:14-30; Luke 12:16-21; Romans 13:6-8; II Corinthians 9:6-15; I Timothy 6; Philippians 4:19

Forgiveness

Proverbs 17:9; Matthew 6:14, 15; 18:21-35; Mark 11:25, 26; Ephesians 4:32; Colossians 2:12, 13; I John 1:8-10

Grief

Psalm 23; Proverbs 10:28; John 11:33-36; 14:1-6; I Corinthians 15; II Corinthians 5:1-8; I Thessalonians 4:13-18

Guilt

Psalm 73; Isaiah 26:3, 4; 53:6; John 8:8-11; Romans 3:23-26; 6:23; II Corinthians 7:8-10; I John 1:8-10; 3:18; 5:4-15

Illness

Psalm 103:3; John 9:2; I Corinthians 11:29, 30; II Corinthians 12:7-10; James 1:2-4

Loneliness

Genesis 2:18; Psalm 139; Proverbs 17:17; 18:24; Romans 8:26-31, 35-39; I John 4:13

Lust

Exodus 20:17; Matthew 5:27, 28; Romans 13:13, 14; Galatians 5:16-26; Ephesians 2:3; Titus 2:11-14; James 1:13-16; I Peter 1:13-16; I John 2:15, 16

Preparing for Marriage

Genesis 2:21-25; Proverbs 18:22; Matthew 5:31, 32; 19:3-12; I Corinthians 7:1-5, 24-40; Ephesians 5:22-33; Colossians 3:18, 19; Hebrews 13:4; I Peter 3:1-17

Pride

Proverbs 8:13; 11:2; 13:10; 16:18; 18:12

Sexual Problems

Genesis 19; Leviticus 18:22, 23; Matthew 5:27, 28; Romans 1:26-32; I Corinthians 6:9-11; Galatians 5:24; Titus 2:11-15; I Peter 2:11; Jude 16-21

Stealing

Exodus 20:15; Proverbs 29:24; Ephesians 4:28

Stewardship of Talents and of Time

Matthew 25:14-30; Luke 12:15-21; Romans 12:3-8; I Corinthians 12

Student/Parent Relations

Genesis 18:19; Exodus 20:12 Deuteronomy 6:6-25; I Samuel 15:22, 23; Ephesians 6:1-4; Hebrews 5:8, 9; I Peter 1:22

Subjection to Authority

Romans 13:1-7; Ephesians 5:6, 21-23; Colossians 4:1; I Timothy 5:1, 2; 6:1, 3, 4; Hebrews 13:17

Appendix F List of Test Publishers

American College Testing Program
(ACT)
P.O. Box 168
Iowa City, Iowa 52240

American Guidance Service, Inc.
720 Washington Avenue SE
Minneapolis, Minnesota 55414

The Bobbs-Merrill Co., Inc.
Box 558
4300 West 62nd Street
Indianapolis, Indiana 46206

Bureau of Educational Research and Service
University of Iowa
Iowa City, Iowa 52240

College Entrance Examination Board
(CEEB)
888 Seventh Avenue
New York, New York 10019
Order Department: Box 2815
Princeton, New Jersey 08541

Consulting Psychologists Press, Inc.
577 College Avenue
Palo Alto, California 94306

CTB/McGraw-Hill
Del Monte Research Park
Monterey, California 93940

Educational and Industrial Testing Service
P.O. Box 7234
San Diego, California 92107

Educational Testing Service
(ETS)
Rosedale Road
Princeton, New Jersey 08540

Harcourt Brace Jovanovich, Inc.
757 Third Avenue
New York, New York 10017

Houghton Mifflin Company
One Beacon Street
Boston, Massachusetts 02107

Institute for Personality and Ability Testing
1602 Coronado Drive
Champaign, Illinois 61820

Personnel Press
191 Spring Street
Lexington, Massachusetts 02173

The Psychological Corporation
757 Third Avenue
New York, New York 10017

Psychological Test Specialists
Box 1441
Missoula, Montana 59801

Psychometric Affiliates
1743 Monterey
Chicago, Illinois 60643

Science Research Association, Inc.
155 North Wacker Drive
Chicago, Illinois 60606

Sheridan Psychological Services, Inc.
P.O. Box 6101
Orange, California 92667

C.H. Stoelting
424 North Homan Avenue
Chicago, Illinois 60624

Teachers College Press
Teachers College, Columbia University
1234 Amsterdam Avenue
New York, New York 10027

Western Psychological Services
12031 Wilshire Boulevard
Los Angeles, California 90025

Appendix G Predicting Student Enrollment

Planning future school programs, budgeting, and determining staff needs all require some knowledge of future enrollment. Of course there is no known way to determine future enrollment with certainty, if a basic history of enrollment is available for five or more years, it is possible to make estimates that are statistically significant. These estimates are calculated with the assumption that certain given factors that interacted to impact enrollment during the past decade will continue to interact in the same manner.

The forecast method suggested below is based on linear correlation (commonly called the "least squares" method) of two lines of regression. The formula frequently used is:

$Y_p = a + bX$ where Y_p = predicted enrollment; X = deviation from the base year from which the prediction is being made; $a + b$ = constants to be derived as follows:

$$a = \frac{\Sigma Y}{N} \qquad b = \frac{\Sigma XY}{\Sigma X^2}$$

In using this formula we must always have an odd number of years. A minimum of five years is suggested; however, three may be used. Always use the greatest number of years possible. The median (middle) year becomes the base.

In the following example, SY = school year; X = deviation from the base year; Y = enrollment for the school year; XY = product of the deviation and enrollment; X^2 = square of the deviation; and N = number of years for which data are used.

SY	X	Y	XY	X^2
1974/75	-5	249	-1,245	25
1975/76	-4	313	-1,252	16
1976/77	-3	359	-1,077	9
1977/78	-2	391	-782	4
1978/79	-1	425	-425	1
1979/80	0	461	0	0
1980/81	1	475	475	1
1981/82	2	492	984	4
1982/83	3	512	1,536	9
1983/84	4	561	2,244	16
1984/85	5	585	2,925	25
	Y=	ΣY = 4,823	ΣXY = 3,383	110

$$a = \frac{4823}{11} = 438.45 \qquad b = \frac{3383}{110} = 30.75$$

The enrollment for the school year 1985/86 can be calculated in the following way:

$$Y_p = a + bX = 438.45 + 30.75(6) = 622.95$$

Any year can be calculated by substituting the deviation from the base year for X. We could calculate the enrollment for the 1986/87 school year by substituting the number 7 for X.

Advantages of the "least squares" method of enrollment projection are these:

1. It makes use of data readily available and does not require extensive record keeping.

2. It is a proven mathematical process for prediction based solely on past enrollment.

3. The accuracy of the prediction can be measured mathematically.

Disadvantages of this method are these:

1. It is completely dependent on an adequate and accurate amount of historical data to establish trends.

2. The system is more appropriate to populations large enough to exhibit a steady trend.

3. The system cannot accommodate any extraneous factors (such as socioeconomic change) which will alter enrollments. If such factors are foreseen, the derived projections must be modified by subjective judgment.

4. Although valuable as indicators, projections far into the future are of doubtful reliablity since exponential changes (rising birth rates, city growth, etc.) cannot be included until they are reflected in the historical data.

Forecast of Teacher Needs

To use enrollment predictions to forecast the number of teachers required in the future, the following formula may be helpful:

$T = \dfrac{E}{P}$ where T = teachers; E = enrollment; P = pupil/teacher ratio desired.

Assuming the desired pupil/teacher ratio is 30/1, the number of teachers needed for the 1985/86 school year could be calculated as follows:

$$T = \frac{623}{30} = 20.77 \text{ which would normally be rounded to 21.}$$

Appendix H Sample Student Record

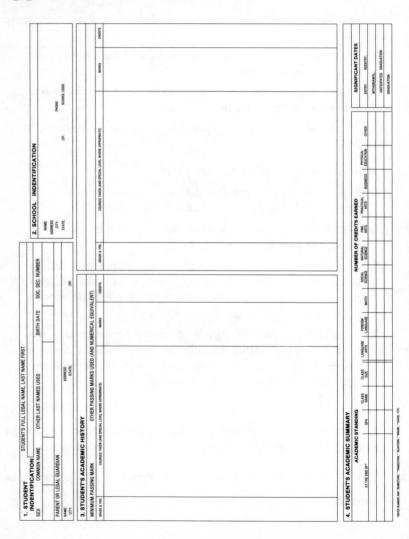

5. ADDITIONAL STUDENT INFORMATION

STUDENT'S NAME, LAST NAME FIRST

Additional information about this student as checked below, is provided either in this space or on an attached pages

☐ A Interests, activities, and achievements   ☐ B Special features of student's program   ☐ C Special problems or needs   ☐ D Personal inventory or checklist   ☐ E Written comments   ☐ F Other _____

6. TEST SCORES *(PRIMARILY GRADES 10-12)*

7. ADDITIONAL SCHOOL INFORMATION

Additional information about our school, as checked below, is provided on the attached pages or school profile.

☐ A Accreditation information   ☐ C Method of computing class rank   ☐ E Explanation of curriculum   ☐ G Frequency distribution
☐ B Method of computing GPA   ☐ D Key to symbols and titles   ☐ F Description of marking system   ☐ H Other

8. PREVIOUS SECONDARY SCHOOLS ATTENDED

NAME OF SCHOOL	STREET ADDRESS	CITY	STATE	ZIP	FROM			TO		
					MONTH	YEAR		MONTH	YEAR	

9. SCHOOL OFFICIALS

SCHOOL PRINCIPAL	PERSON TO CONTACT FOR ADDITIONAL INFORMATION	SIGNATURE OF OFFICIAL CERTIFYING THIS TRANSCRIPT *(School Seal if Available)*
NAME: _____	NAME: _____	NAME: _____
TITLE: _____	TITLE: _____	DATE: _____

This Secondary School Record was designed to assist schools in complying with the federal law on open access to records. The 1975 edition was developed cooperatively by AACJC, AACRAO, APGA, ASCA, NACAC, NAIS, NCEA, and NASSP, with the assistance of ACT, CEEB, and ETS. Reprinted with the permission of NASSP.

Appendix I Carbonless Report Card Sets

THUNDER MOUNTAIN CHRISTIAN SCHOOL

Kindergarten

Student's _____ Teacher _____ Year _____

	Quarters	1	2	3	4
Bible Memory Verses					
Letter Recognition (1st Sem.)					
Phonics					
Reading (2nd Sem.)					
Comprehension					
Printing Letters					
Printing Numbers					
Math Concepts					
Uses Language Skills					
Listens & Follows Directions					
Completes Tasks					
Respects & Obeys Authority					

	Quarters	1	2	3	4
Is Courteous					
Demonstrates Self-discipline					
Plays Well with Others					
Has Cheerful Attitude					
Co-ordination & Development of Perceptual Skills					
Coloring					
Pasting & Cutting					
Displays Self-confidence					
General Conduct					

Days Tardy . . . .
Days Absent . . . .
Days Present . . . .
Days on Roll . . . .

Grading Scale:
1 . . . . Superior
2 . . . . Excellent
3 . . . . Above Average
4 . . . . Average
5 . . . . Below Average
6 . . . . Unsatisfactory

152

THUNDER MOUNTAIN CHRISTIAN SCHOOL

Grades 1-8

Student's _____ Teacher _____ Grade _____ Year _____

	Quarters				Final
	1	2	3	4	
Bible					
Conduct					
Reading					
Spelling/Phonics (Grade 1)					
Spelling (Grades 2-6)					
Penmanship					
Math					
English					
U.S. History					
World History					
Civics					

	Quarters				Final
	1	2	3	4	
Georgia History					
U.S. Geography					
World Geography					
Biological Science					
Elementary Science					
Earth Science					
Music					
Physical Education					
Chorus (Grades 7-8)					
Band (Grades 7-8)					

	1	2	3	4
Days Tardy				
Days Absent				
Days Present				
Days on Roll				

Date Enrolled _____ Achievement Test _____

Date Withdrawn _____ Percentile _____

Finished School Year Yes _____ No _____

Assigned To _____ Grade for Next School Year _____

Conference Requested Yes _____ No _____

EXPLANATION OF GRADING

A - 93-100 Superior
B - 85-92   Excellent
C - 75-84   Above Average
D - 70-74   Average
F - 69-below Below Average

153

THUNDER MOUNTAIN CHRISTIAN SCHOOL

Grades 9-12

Student's Name _____ Teacher _____ Grade _____ Year _____

	Units	QUARTERS 1	2	3	4	Final
Demerits						
Bible						
English						
English						
Speech / Drama						
Journalism						
History						
United States I, II						
World History						
American Government						
Math						
Algebra I, II						
General Math						
Geometry						
Advanced Math						
Music						
Chorus						
Band						

	Units	QUARTERS 1	2	3	4	Final
Science						
Physical Science						
Biology						
Chemistry						
Physics						
Business						
Business Math						
Accounting						
Typing I, II						
Shorthand						
Office Practice						
Computers						
Language						
Spanish I, II						
Mechanical Drawing						
Physical Education						

EXPLANATION OF GRADING

	1	2	3	4
Days Tardy				
Days Absent				
Days Present				
Days on Roll				

A — 93-100 Superior
B — 85-92 Above Average
C — 75-84 Average
D — 70-74 Poor
F — 69-below Failure

CONDUCT EVALUATION
1 — Exceptional
2 — Adequate
3 — Inadequate

Date Enrolled _____

Date Withdrawn _____

Finished School Year Yes _____ No _____

Assigned To _____ Grade for Next School Year

Conference Requested Yes _____ No _____

Total Credits _____

Achievement Test
Percentile _____

Appendix J School Profile

Thunder Mountain Christian School
1000 Waterway Blvd.
Anytown, CO 76432

John Q. Sample, EdD, Principal
Dorothy N. Counsel, M. S., Guidance Counselor
(803) 436-0101

Thunder Mountain Christian School is a ministry of Anytown Bible Church. The school's primary purpose is to assist Christian parents in training their children in accordance with Scripture; thus, fulfilling the biblical mandate "Train up a child in the way he should go" (Proverbs 22:6a). The entire program of the school is directed toward shaping the child in "the image of His Son."

Thunder Mountain Christian School was founded as a ministry of the church in 1967. Kindergarten through grade twelve is now offered. The first graduating class was in 1974. Enrollment for 1983/84 was 661 with a graduating class of 42. Over the last five years, 87 percent of the graduating class went on to some form of higher education.

The school year is 180 days of six hours duration. The school year begins on the Monday before Labor Day each year. Conventional classroom instruction is offered at all levels. The pupil/teacher ratio is approximately 22 to 1.

The professional school staff includes the principal, two vice-principals, a guidance counselor and 33 classroom teachers. All administrative staff hold the master's degree as a minimum; 30 percent of the classroom teachers have the master's degree in their specialization. All teachers are assigned within their area of academic preparation.

A cumulative grade point average (GPA) is calculated for academic subjects on the basis of grades earned in grades 9 - 12. Class rank is derived directly from these GPAs with equal weight given to all subjects of equal unit value.

Marking system:

A	93—100	Superior
B	85—92	Above average
C	75—84	Average
D	65—74	Passing
F	below 65	Failing

Class rank is determined at the end of the Junior year and again upon completion of graduation requirements. All subjects for which a letter grade is assigned are included in the computation.

Graduation requirements:

English	4 units
Social Studies	3 units
Foreign language	1 unit
Science	2 units
Mathematics	2 units
Bible	4 units (at least one each year enrolled at school)
Physical education	2 units
Electives	4 units
	22 units

All Seniors are required to take the American College Test. For the last five years the average score has been 20.3 which is equivalent to the 62 percentile.

Appendix K Sample Transcript Form

THUNDER MOUNTAIN CHRISTIAN SCHOOL

1000 Waterway Blvd.
Anytown, CO 76432

STUDENT'S NAME _____ Last _____ First _____ Middle _____ Student No. _____

HOME ADDRESS _____ Street and Number _____ City _____ State _____ Zip _____

GENERAL INFORMATION

DATE OF ENTRANCE _____ DATE OF BIRTH _____
PLACE OF BIRTH _____
SEX _____ RACE _____ CITIZENSHIP _____
DENOMINATION _____
FATHER, STEPFATHER, GUARDIAN _____
ADDRESS _____

FATHER'S OCCUPATION _____
FATHER'S CITIZENSHIP _____ LIVING? _____
MOTHER OR STEPMOTHER _____
ADDRESS _____

MOTHER'S OCCUPATION _____ FATHER'S _____ LIVING? _____
NATIONALITY: MOTHER'S _____
NO. BROTHERS _____ NO. SISTERS _____ LIVING WITH _____
SCHOOL LAST ATTENDED _____
ADDRESS _____

OCCUPATIONAL AND EDUCATIONAL INTENTIONS

COLLEGE CHOICE FIRST _____
SECOND _____
OCCUPATIONAL INTENTION _____

PERSONAL TRAITS

SYMBOLS 5-HIGH. 4-ABOVE AVG 3-AVG 2-BELOW AVG 1-LOW

	YEAR		
ACCURACY			
CO-OPERATION			
INDUSTRY			
LEADERSHIP			
APPEARANCE			
RELIABILITY			

KEY TO GRADING SYSTEM

A—Superior, 94-100; B—Above Average, 86-93; C—Average, 78-85; D—Passing, 70-77; F—Failure, 0-69; I—Incomplete; P—Pass; W—Withdrawn; X—Absent from examination. Credit is based on achievement grade, C-Grade recommended for College. One unit represents five recitations a week, 55 minutes in length for 36 weeks. Eighteen units are required for graduation.

SUBJECT	ACHIEVEMENT	EFFORT	ACHIEVEMENT	EFFORT	UNITS

SUBJECT	ACHIEVEMENT	EFFORT	ACHIEVEMENT	EFFORT	UNITS

Was graduated _____ Ranked _____ in class of _____

TEST RECORD

DATE	NAME OF TEST	RESULTS

ACHIEVEMENT PERCENTILE SCORES

Math	Wn. Exp.	So Stu.	Sci.

ATTENDANCE SUMMARY

YEAR	DAYS ABSENT	PER. TARDY	YEAR	DAYS ABSENT	PER. TARDY

CO-CURRICULAR RECORD

YEAR	ACTIVITY, HONOR, OR OFFICE

(SEAL)

_____ PRINCIPAL

_____ DATE

157

Appendix K

TRANSCRIPTS ISSUED	DATE

THUNDER MOUNTAIN CHRISTIAN SCHOOL

1000 Waterway Blvd.
Anytown, CO 76432

PERMANENT RECORD
Page 1 of 2

KEY TO SYMBOLS

[F] Final Grade   [U] Carnegie Units
(A) 93 - 100% Superior   (B) 85 - 92% Above Average
(C) 75 - 84% Average   (D) 65 - 74% Poor
(F) 64 - below Failure

Name _____ Birthdate _____

GRADE	19___	19___		GRADE	19___	19___		GRADE	19___	19___
SCHOOL				SCHOOL				SCHOOL		

SUBJECT	1	2	3	4	F	U	SUBJECT	1	2	3	4	F	U	SUBJECT	1	2	3	4	F	U
CONDUCT							CONDUCT							CONDUCT						
PRESENT							PRESENT							PRESENT						
TARDY							TARDY							TARDY						
ON ROLL							ON ROLL							ON ROLL						

GRADE	19___	19___		GRADE	19___	19___		GRADE	19___	19___
SCHOOL				SCHOOL				SCHOOL		

SUBJECT	1	2	3	4	F	U	SUBJECT	1	2	3	4	F	U	SUBJECT	1	2	3	4	F	U
CONDUCT							CONDUCT							CONDUCT						
PRESENT							PRESENT							PRESENT						
TARDY							TARDY							TARDY						
ON ROLL							ON ROLL							ON ROLL						

SUMMER SESSION	19___		SUMMER SESSION	19___		SUMMER SESSION	19___
SCHOOL			SCHOOL			SCHOOL	

SUBJECT				F	U	SUBJECT				F	U	SUBJECT				F	U

Appendix K

<u>SUMMARY OF HIGH SCHOOL CREDITS</u>

SUBJECT	UNITS	SUBJECT	UNITS
ENGLISH/LITERATURE		MATH	
U.S. HISTORY		FOREIGN LANGUAGE	
U.S. GOVERNMENT/CONSTITUTION		TYPING	
OTHER SOCIAL STUDIES		MUSIC	
BIOLOGY		BIBLE	
OTHER SCIENCE		OTHER ELECTIVES	

One unit of credit is earned by successfully completing a class that meets for 50 minutes daily for 36 weeks or the equivalent. Fractional units are given for classes meeting for shorter periods. A minimum final grade of D is required to receive credit for a course. Eighth grade students permitted to carry high school level courses will be awarded unit credit for those courses they satisfactorily complete. All high school level courses are indicated by unit credits.

ACTIVITIES

HONORS

STANDARDIZED TESTING

GRADUATED_____

RANKED_____ IN CLASS OF _____

THIS TRANSCRIPT IS NOT OFFICIAL UNLESS SIGNED BY THE PRINCIPAL AND SEALED.

THUNDER MOUNTAIN CHRISTIAN SCHOOL

1000 Waterway Blvd.   Anytown, CO 76432

Appendix L Professional Journals

American Psychologist
1400 North Uhle Street
Arlington, VA 22201 $50

Christian Educators Journal
1500 Cornell Drive, SE
Grand Rapids, MI 49506 $4

Counselor Education and Supervision
5999 Stevenson Avenue
Alexandria, VA 22304 $12

Education
1362 Santa Cruz City
Chula Vista, CA 92010 $15

Educational & Psychological Measurement
Box 6907
College Station
Durham, NC 27708 $50

Education Digest
Box 8623
Ann Arbor, MI 48107 $15

Elementary School Guidance & Counseling
5999 Stevenson Avenue
Alexandria, VA 22304 $20

Journal of Counseling Psychology
1200 17th Street, NW
Washington, DC 20036 $35

Journal of Counseling Services
Louisiana State University
Peabody Hall, Department of Education
Baton Rouge, LA 70803   free

Personnel & Guidance Journal
5999 Stevenson Avenue
Alexandria, VA 22304 $32

Phi Delta Kappan
Eighth & Union
P.O. Box 789
Bloomington, IN 47402 $20

Psychology Today
P.O. Box 2562
Boulder, CO 80321 $15

The School Counselor
5999 Stevenson Avenue
Alexandria, VA 22304 $25

Vocational Guidance Quarterly
5999 Stevenson Avenue
Alexandria, VA 22304 $12

The fact that these periodicals are being listed as references does not mean that Bob Jones University or the author of this book endorses their contents from the standpoint of morals, philosophy, theology, or scientific hypotheses. Because of the scarcity of materials available on Christian education, it is sometimes necessary to use portions of materials the contents of which we cannot wholly endorse.

Bibliography

Adams, J. E. (1970). *Competent to counsel.* Grand Rapids, MI: Baker.

Adams, J. E. (1973). *The Christian counselor's manual.* Grand Rapids, MI: Baker.

Adams, J. E. (1975). *The use of Scriptures in counseling.* Grand Rapids, MI: Baker.

Adams, J. E. (1977). *Helps for counselors.* Grand Rapids, MI: Baker.

Adams, J. E. (1979). *More than redemption.* Phillipsburg, NJ: Presbyterian and Reformed.

Adams, J. E. (1981). *Ready to restore.* Phillipsburg, NJ: Presbyterian and Reformed.

Adams, J. E. (1982). *What to do on Thursday.* Phillipsburg, NJ: Presbyterian and Reformed.

Baird, C. G. (1983). *The power of a positive self-image.* Wheaton, IL: Victor.

Bradley, J. D. (1977). *Christian career planning.* Portland, OR: Multnomah.

Brookover, W. B., & Erickson, E. L. (1975). *Sociology of education.* Homewood, IL: Dorsey.

Brookover, W. B., Erickson, E. L., & Joiner, L. (1967). *Concept of ability and school achievement III* (Report of Cooperative Research Project 2831). East Lansing: Michigan State University, Bureau of Publication Services.

Blood, D. F., & Budd, W. C. (1972). *Educational measurement and evaluation.* New York: Harper.

Coleman, J. C. (1960). *Personality dynamics and affective behavior.* Chicago: Scott, Foresman.

The College Board. (1983). *Academic preparation for college: What students need to know and be able to do.* New York: Author.

The College Board. (1984). *Academic preparation for the world of work.* New York: Author.

Collins, G. R. (1973). *Overcoming anxiety.* Santa Ana, CA: Vision.

Collins, G. R. (1980). *Christian counseling.* Waco, TX: Word.

Crane, W. E. (1970). *Where God comes in: The divine "plus" in counseling.* Waco, TX: Word.

Deuink, J. W., & Herbster, C. D. (1982). *Effective Christian school management.* Greenville, SC: Bob Jones Univ. Press.

Dobson, J. (1970). *Dare to discipline.* Wheaton, IL: Tyndale.

Dobson, J. (1974). *Hide or seek.* Old Tappan, NJ: Revel.

Dobson, J. (1978). *Preparing for adolescence.* Santa Ana, CA: Vision.

Dobson, J. (1978). *The strong-willed child.* Wheaton, IL: Tyndale.

Ebel, R. L. (1977). *The uses of standardized testing* (Fastback 93). Bloomington, IN: Phi Delta Kappa.

Ebel, R. L. (1979). *Essentials of educational measurement* (3rd ed.). Englewoods Cliffs, NJ: Prentice-Hall.

Getz, G. A. (1976). *Building up one another.* Wheaton, IL: Victor.

Kennedy, E. (1977). *On becoming a counselor: A basic guide for non-professional counselors.* New York: Seabury.

Lyman, H. B. (1978). *Test scores and what they mean.* Englewood Cliffs, NJ: Prentice-Hall.

Meier, P. D., Minirth, F. B., & Wichern, F. (1982). *Introduction to psychology and counseling: Christian perspectives and applications.* Grand Rapids, MI: Baker.

Mendelsohn, R. D., Brookover, W. B., & Erickson, E. L. (1972). *Teacher credibility and parental involvement in school related activities.* Paper presented at the American Educational Research Association, Chicago, IL.

National Association of Secondary School Principals. (1972). *Rank in class.* Reston, VA: Author.

National Association of Secondary School Principals. (1974). School to college transcripts. *Curriculum Report, 3* (5) Author.

Perrone, V. (1977). *The abuses of standardized testing* (Fastback 92). Bloomington, IN: Phi Delta Kappa.

Purkey, W. W. (1970). *Self-concept and school achievement.* Englewood Cliffs, NJ: Prentice-Hall.

Purkey, W. W. (1978). *Inviting school success.* Belmont, CA: Wadsworth.

Solomon, C. R. (1971). *Handbook to happiness.* Wheaton, IL: Tyndale.

Shertzer, B. & Stone, S. C. (1981). *Fundamentals of Guidance* (4th ed.). Boston: Houghton Mifflin.

Wright, N., & Inman, M. A. (1978). *A guidebook to dating, waiting, and choosing a mate.* Irvine, CA: Harvest House.

The fact that these materials are being listed as references does not mean that Bob Jones University or the author of this book endorses their contents from the standpoint of morals, philosophy, theology, or scientific hypotheses. Because of the scarcity of materials available on Christian education, it is sometimes necessary to use portions of books the contents of which we cannot wholly endorse.